tapestry bead crochet
projects & techniques

Ann Benson

LARK CRAFTS

An Imprint of Sterling Publishing Co., Inc.
New York

WWW.LARKCRAFTS.COM

Content Team Leader, Jewelry/Beading
Ray Hemachandra

Editor
Larry Shea

Art Director
Megan Kirby

Art Assistant
Jeff Hamilton

Graphics and Illustrations
Ann Benson

Photography Director
Dana Irwin

Photographers
Stewart O'Shields and Ann Benson

Cover Designer
Celia Naranjo

Project on previous page
by Lauren Miller.

Library of Congress Cataloging-in-Publication Data

Benson, Ann.
  Tapestry bead crochet : projects & techniques / Ann Benson.
      p. cm.
  Includes index.
  ISBN 978-1-60059-337-6 (pb with cd : alk. paper)
  1. Beadwork. 2. Beadwork--Patterns. 3. Crocheting. I. Title.
  TT860.B4865 2010
  745.58'2--dc22

                                              2010003893

10 9 8 7 6 5 4 3 2

Published by Lark Crafts
An Imprint of Sterling Publishing Co., Inc.
387 Park Avenue South, New York, NY 10016

Text © 2010, Ann Benson
Photography © 2010, Lark Crafts, an Imprint of Sterling Publishing Co., Inc.,
unless otherwise specified
Graphics and Illustrations © 2010, Ann Benson

Distributed in Canada by Sterling Publishing,
c/o Canadian Manda Group, 165 Dufferin Street
Toronto, Ontario, Canada M6K 3H6

Distributed in the United Kingdom by GMC Distribution Services,
Castle Place, 166 High Street, Lewes, East Sussex, England BN7 1XU

Distributed in Australia by Capricorn Link (Australia) Pty Ltd.,
P.O. Box 704, Windsor, NSW 2756 Australia

If you have questions or comments about this book, please contact:
Lark Crafts, 67 Broadway, Asheville, NC 28801, 828-253-0467

Manufactured in China

ISBN 13: 978-1-60059-337-6

For information about custom editions, special sales, premium
and corporate purchases, please contact Sterling Special Sales
Department at 800-805-5489 or specialsales@sterlingpub.com.

For information about desk and examination copies available to
college and university professors, requests must be submitted to
academic@larkbooks.com. Our complete policy can be found
at www.larkcrafts.com.

tapestry bead crochet

introduction

You may already be spellbound by beads, held in thrall to their color and shine.
And you may already understand the grace and beauty of crochet. But put the two
together… well, that's when the magic begins.

This book examines the materials, techniques, and tricks that all come together in a sweet form of artistry—tapestry bead crochet—a craft that can look both traditional and contemporary. I've taken inspiration from beaded crochet bags from the Victorian era and ranging on into the 1920s, and given the look my own aesthetic twist to make it modern and fresh. I've used a lot more imagery than what you see on vintage pieces, and in completely different color schemes than our forebears would have used. Furthermore, I've included a few types of objects that would never have

been made by the beaders of yore—a case for a music player, for example, and another for sunglasses.

I cast a wide net in terms of project designs. You have so many choices: napkin rings, a leopard-print pillbox hat that Zsa-Zsa Gabor would die to own, and a little round box for hiding your treasures. Assert yourself as the mistress of your household with a chatelaine for storing your keys. Or make more bags than you can use in a week, if you changed purses every day.

In the first few chapters, I'll tell you about the many different types of beads, and show you how they can

work together with fiber to bring out the best in both. I'll teach you some fundamental crochet, in case you need that information, and then explain all the techniques necessary to achieve the different parts of the projects.

But do you learn better when someone shows you a technique, instead of telling you how to do it? Most of us do, and I've got you covered by including a 40-minute DVD with this book. Not only does it include footage of how to do tapestry bead crochet; it delves more deeply than the book does into topics such as bead colors, threading, and choosing bag handles.

The bead crochet designs within these pages are simple and quick, and you can progress at your own pace to more challenging pieces. Once you've reached your comfort level, go ahead and design your own graphics using the blank charts provided in the back of the book.

Welcome to the wonderful world of tapestry bead crochet!

Chapter 1
materials and tools

As you work with tapestry bead crochet, you'll discover endless variety in color, style, and design from which to create. Luckily, you won't have to gather an endless list of materials and tools to do so. Beads, thread, hooks, needles, scissors, pliers—that about covers it. Here's everything you need to gather before starting.

seed beads

All the projects in this book are created with a base of glass seed beads. A few larger beads are used for decoration here and there, but the vast majority of your crocheting will be done with size 11° seed beads. These beads are manufactured in both Japan and the Czech Republic. You'll find distinct differences in size and shape between the beads that come from these two countries.

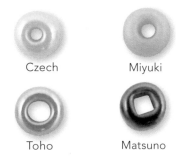

Czech   Miyuki

Toho   Matsuno

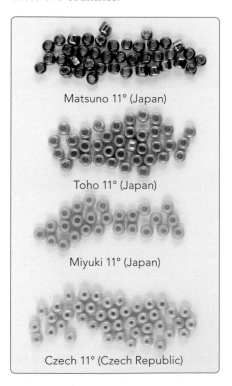

Matsuno 11° (Japan)

Toho 11° (Japan)

Miyuki 11° (Japan)

Czech 11° (Czech Republic)

Czech seed beads are quite oval in shape, with smoothly rounded surfaces. The country has several prominent bead manufacturers; between them, they make a huge variety of colors and finishes. Czech seed beads are usually strung into hanks at the factories, with multiple hanks tied together to form a kilo. More often than not, though, you'll find them repackaged for sale in tubes or bags of a smaller gram weight, usually in the range of 10 to 20 grams.

Japanese seed beads are often sold by the name of their manufacturer, such as Miyuki or Toho. In the bead lists in this book, Japanese beads will always include a manufacturer's or brand name, while Czech beads will be referred to as just that: "Czech beads."

The holes in Czech beads tend to be on the small side. Japanese seed beads, on the other hand, have larger holes. They usually are a bit more squared in shape than Czech beads, and a little larger overall.

bead quantities and varieties

As you begin the projects in this book, you'll be asked to gather beads in quantities such as *Toho #221 11°, dark copper (860 beads)* or *Czech #60014 11°, dark blue (1,240 beads).* You may wonder how you can determine the proper amount of beads to have available. (No, you don't have to count out all the beads before starting!) Just realize that there are approximately 100 beads per gram of Japanese 11° seed beads, and approximately 110 beads per gram of Czech 11° seed beads. When you purchase beads, make sure you'll have plenty on hand for the projects you want to do. The bead counts in this book are precise, but I strongly recommend that you purchase at least 10 percent more than you think you'll need. Any leftover beads may work quite nicely in your next project, or in one down the road.

If you decide to buy hanks of 11° Czech beads, by the way, know that each weighs about 34 to 35 grams; Japanese 11°s don't come on hanks, so don't waste your time searching them out.

If you want to substitute a different bead for one given in a project, you still probably ought to use the same size (most often 11°) and variety of bead (Czech or Japanese). Otherwise, the project elements may not come together properly. You can substitute bead colors, whether you go to a slightly different shade or a completely different hue. I've provided detailed bead information for those who'd like to create projects exactly as pictured, but putting together your bead palette is really up to you.

designing with bead colors and finishes

Color will become an even more important issue when you begin to design your own pieces. Glass beads can be opaque or transparent, or somewhere in between. The color of a bead is the result of a chemical process often involving elements such as zinc, cadmium, or titanium. The base color of a bead is created using a precise mix of silica and a specific element that will produce the desired color in the resulting glass. It's not a dying process, though some beads do have surface dyes. The bead surface can be treated with certain types of finishes to create a specific look. The bead box below shows the same base glass color, treated with four different finishes.

You'll find hundreds, maybe thousands, of colors and finishes available in size 11° seed beads. It's not possible to describe them all, but here are a few important things to remember in choosing your beads:

1 You can mix Japanese and Czech beads within the same design, but use your own design sense to decide if their size differences will matter. As you work more with the two different types of seed beads, you'll develop a feel for how they'll crochet. In most cases, combining Japanese and Czech beads won't have much of an effect on the outcome of your project, though some of the designs in this book include both types in their recommended bead lists.

2 Be aware of the finish on your beads, as they will be subjected to wear. Certain finishes—particularly galvanized finishes—can be unstable, and they may rub off over time. This outcome is often related to the individual user's body chemistry or cosmetics, but there's no way to predict it in advance. The one exception to this rule is stable-finish galvanized beads, in which the finish is more durable. Dyed beads may fade over time, though most manufacturers claim a 30-year color life. Because you're making an heirloom (yes, you are!), you may want to avoid dyed beads as well.

3 Beads that have been electroplated with precious metals are usually fairly stable in finish. You can also find some newer galvanized finishes that wear better, so be sure to determine this when buying your beads. Having a chat with a knowledgeable bead seller about the qualities of their beads is always a good idea.

Galvanized

Matte galvanized

Electroplated

Metal-through

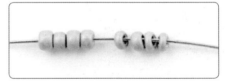

Beads too narrow

Beads too wide

4 Go for consistency as much as you can. Even within one color of the exact same bead, the sizes will be slightly inconsistent. This variation is a natural result of the bead-manufacturing process and doesn't indicate poor quality. As you thread your beads onto the fiber, avoid picking up beads that are obviously larger, smaller, flatter, wider, or irregularly shaped.

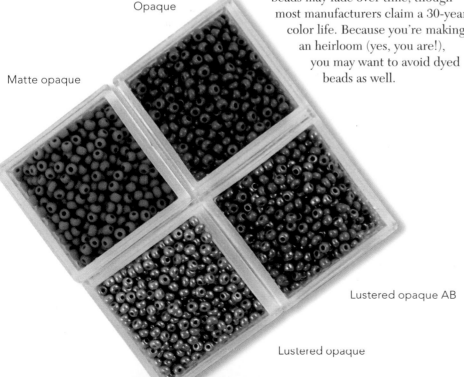

Opaque

Matte opaque

Lustered opaque AB

Lustered opaque

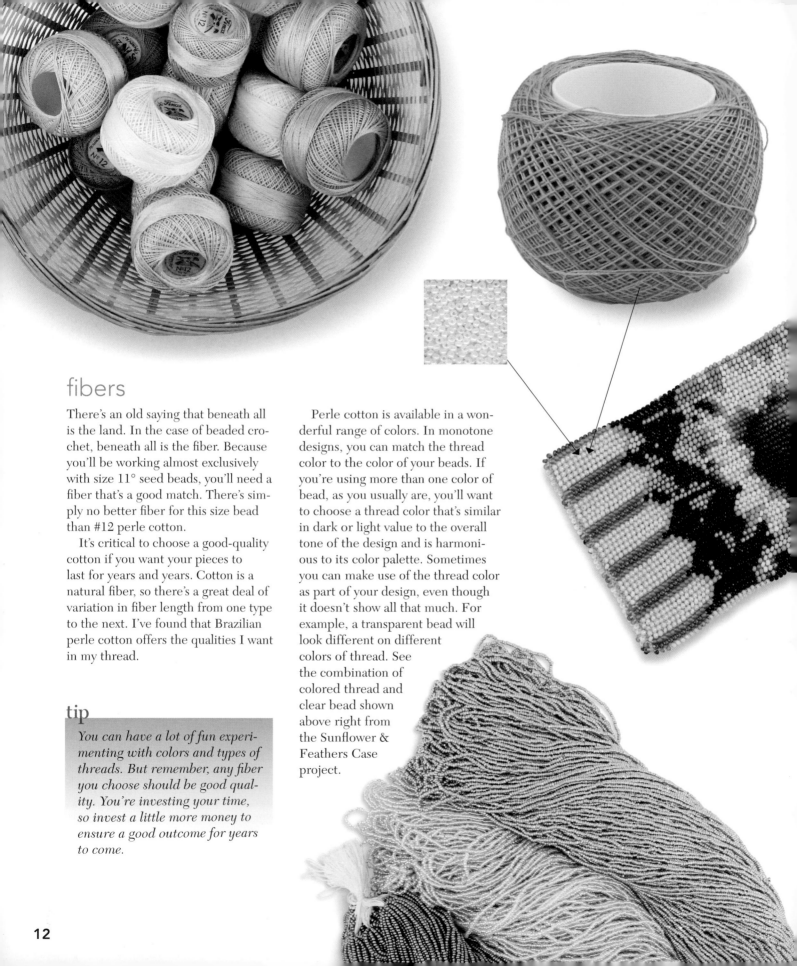

fibers

There's an old saying that beneath all is the land. In the case of beaded crochet, beneath all is the fiber. Because you'll be working almost exclusively with size 11° seed beads, you'll need a fiber that's a good match. There's simply no better fiber for this size bead than #12 perle cotton.

It's critical to choose a good-quality cotton if you want your pieces to last for years and years. Cotton is a natural fiber, so there's a great deal of variation in fiber length from one type to the next. I've found that Brazilian perle cotton offers the qualities I want in my thread.

Perle cotton is available in a wonderful range of colors. In monotone designs, you can match the thread color to the color of your beads. If you're using more than one color of bead, as you usually are, you'll want to choose a thread color that's similar in dark or light value to the overall tone of the design and is harmonious to its color palette. Sometimes you can make use of the thread color as part of your design, even though it doesn't show all that much. For example, a transparent bead will look different on different colors of thread. See the combination of colored thread and clear bead shown above right from the Sunflower & Feathers Case project.

tip

You can have a lot of fun experimenting with colors and types of threads. But remember, any fiber you choose should be good quality. You're investing your time, so invest a little more money to ensure a good outcome for years to come.

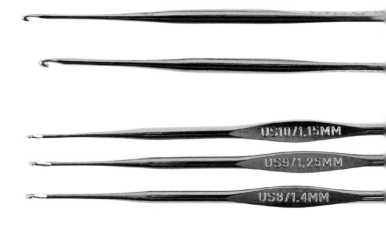

tools

As with just about any task, the right tool will make your crochet work easier, more successful, and just plain more fun.

crochet hooks

The crochet hook is the single most important tool you'll use. All of the designs in this book are worked with steel crochet hooks. I use a size 9 steel crochet hook (1.4 mm) to achieve the desired result. My stitch tension tends to be average, but if you're a type-A crocheter with tight tension, you may want to consider using a size 8 (1.5 mm) hook instead. If your tension is loose, try a size 10 (1.3 mm) hook.

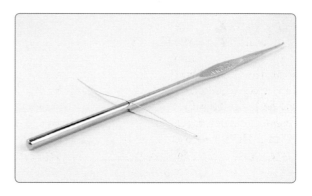

beading needles

You have a number of choices for your threading needle. I use a size 10 long beading needle whenever possible. Embroidery needles have larger eyes than beading needles; these eyes will more easily accommodate the crochet cotton, so you can use embroidery needles as well. The needle you use will really depend on the beads you choose; if the beads have small holes, you'll need a smaller needle.

You can also use a big-eye needle (at right), but over time the needle will deteriorate, so you may need more than one to complete your project. Twisted-wire needles can also be used (below right), but like big-eye needles, they sometimes break down. If you use them, keep a few extra handy.

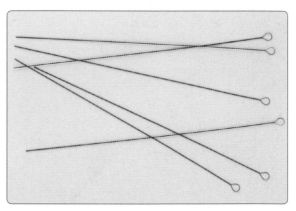

For burying thread ends, you can use a small tapestry needle such as size 24 or 26 (below). The larger eyes are easier to thread. You can also use a dental floss threader to load your beads (above). You'll have no trouble at all getting the fiber through the eye. The floss threader will collapse as you thread the beads over it, so you may need to replace it from time to time.

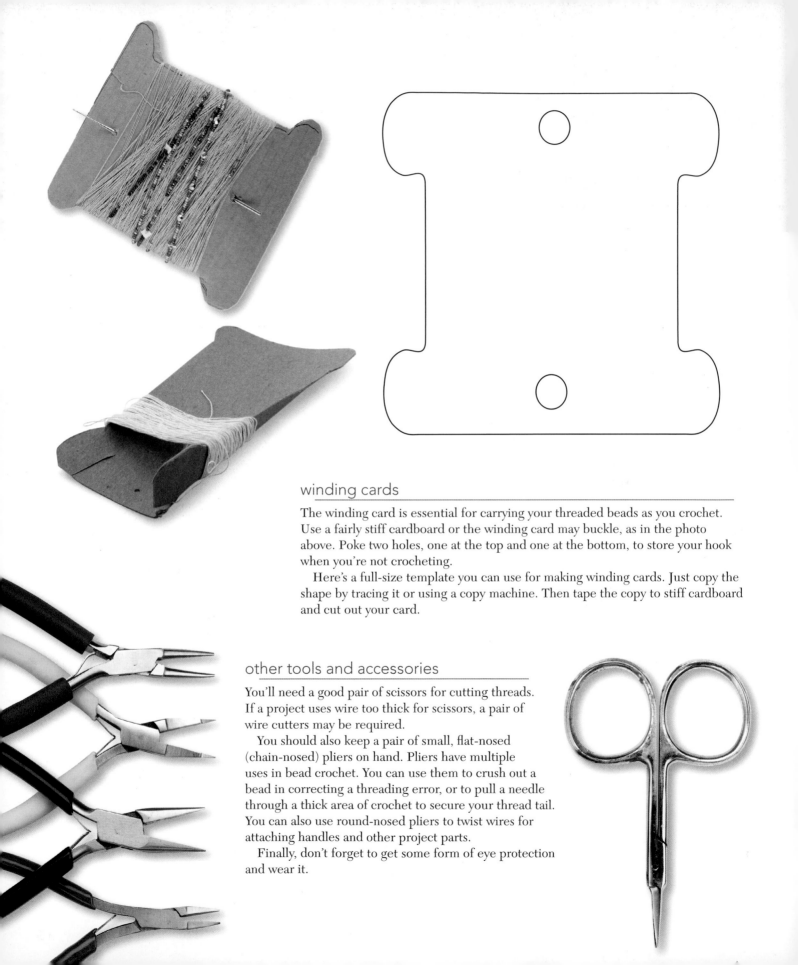

winding cards

The winding card is essential for carrying your threaded beads as you crochet. Use a fairly stiff cardboard or the winding card may buckle, as in the photo above. Poke two holes, one at the top and one at the bottom, to store your hook when you're not crocheting.

Here's a full-size template you can use for making winding cards. Just copy the shape by tracing it or using a copy machine. Then tape the copy to stiff cardboard and cut out your card.

other tools and accessories

You'll need a good pair of scissors for cutting threads. If a project uses wire too thick for scissors, a pair of wire cutters may be required.

You should also keep a pair of small, flat-nosed (chain-nosed) pliers on hand. Pliers have multiple uses in bead crochet. You can use them to crush out a bead in correcting a threading error, or to pull a needle through a thick area of crochet to secure your thread tail. You can also use round-nosed pliers to twist wires for attaching handles and other project parts.

Finally, don't forget to get some form of eye protection and wear it.

Chapter 2
the basic stitches

Now that you have some colorful seed beads and thread on your table and your crochet hook in hand (at least figuratively), you'll want to start putting them to use. In this chapter, we'll review the basic stitches you need to know, first making them without beads and then—and this is where the fun starts—adding beads to your crochet.

getting started

You'll use only three crochet stitches to create the projects in this book: *chain stitch*, which is always the starting foundation; *slip stitch*, an important part of the step-up process; and *single crochet*, which will be used for the bulk of the stitching.

You'll start every project in this book with an unbeaded chain. When you're making a flat design, this chain will likely be the same number of stitches as each round in the design. In shaped designs—for example, those with hex bases or gussets—the number will be different. The instructions for each pattern will give the required number of stitches in the starting chain.

To save space, some of the project instructions use crochet abbreviations. A full chart of the abbreviations used in this book appears on page 128.

chain stitch

All chains start with a slip knot, which counts as the first stitch. Form a ring with your thread, then leave a tail of at least 4 inches (10.2 cm), which you'll bury within the crochet later. (In some designs, you'll be told to leave a longer thread tail, which may be used later in finishing the piece.) Use your hook to pull a loop up from within the ring, then tighten the thread until you have one loop on the hook, with the tail hanging.

chain stitch

making the slip knot

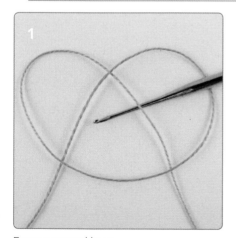

Form a pretzel loop

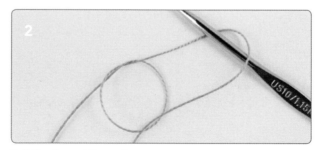

Pull the thread through with the hook

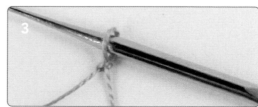

Tighten the thread to complete the slip knot

making a chain

Now wrap the thread around the hook, from front to back over the top, and catch the thread in the hook. Pull the caught thread through the slip knot to form a second chain.

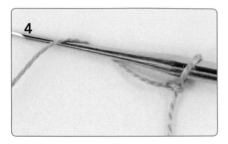

Wrap the thread around the hook

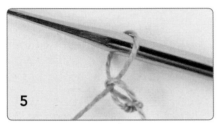

Pull through to form the chain

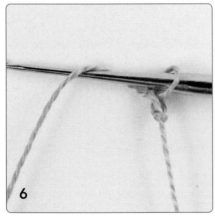

Repeat the wrap and pull to form another chain

Continue in this manner, wrapping the thread around the hook and pulling it through each time. Try to keep the stitches in the chain even. If they're too tight, you'll have trouble stitching into the chain later, and if they're too loose, the edge will have a sloppy appearance. The chains should be as uniform as possible.

untwisting the chain

You'll probably notice that the chain is twisted. This will happen even if you have perfect tension and size uniformity. It's easier, though, to handle an untwisted chain when you're joining the ends together to start your rounds. To straighten and flatten the chain, you can press it with a steam iron.

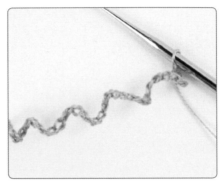

Chain unpressed

Chain pressed

slip stitch

Slip stitch is used mostly in joining. For example, you'll use it when you join one end of the starting chain to the other, or as part of the step-up when you join the completed round together before beginning the next round.

To make a slip stitch, first insert the hook into the stitch you want to join to, then wrap the thread back to front, over the top of the hook.

Next, catch the thread in the hook and pull it through the stitch you're joining to and through the loop on the shaft of the hook. It's important to keep medium tension on slip stitches; even experienced crocheters tend to pull too tightly. This may cause difficulties later, so keep it in mind as you crochet.

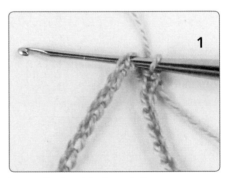

Insert the hook in first chain

Wrap the thread

Pull through both loops to complete the slip stitch

single crochet

Single crochet is the workhorse stitch that carries the beads, which will show on the outside of the work. It forms a neat fabric that can serve nicely as the inside of a bag if you don't want to add a lining.

You'll build single crochet on an existing chain. Before you begin single crochet, join the last chain to the first chain with a slip stitch. As part of the step-up—a technique we'll examine in detail later—you'll make one chain. Now insert the hook into the same chain as the one in which you made your slip stitch. Pull up a loop, then wrap the thread over the hook, from back to front. Pull the thread through both loops on the hook to complete the stitch. This is one unbeaded single crochet.

To make the next one, insert the hook into the next chain, then repeat the same steps.

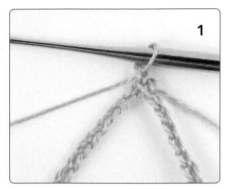

Chain one to start the round

Insert the hook in the same space as the slip stitch

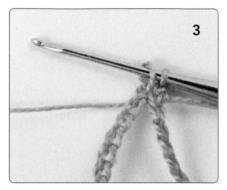

Pull up a loop of thread

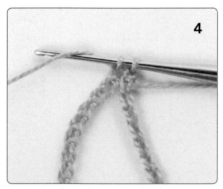

Wrap the thread over the hook from back to front

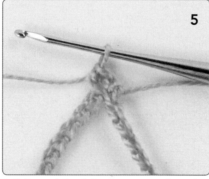

Pull through both loops to complete the single crochet

For each additional single crochet, see the photo above. You'll insert the hook in the next chain, pull up a loop, wrap the thread, and pull through both loops.

Overview of the entire single crochet stitch (without beads)

adding beads in single crochet

Now that we've talked about the second word in "bead crochet," let's bring in the first one. To add a bead, proceed as for unbeaded single crochet until you have the two loops on the hook. Before you wrap the thread around the hook, bring a bead down the thread, and nestle it close to the loops, directly under the hook, as shown at right. Now wrap the thread back to front over the top of the hook; catch the thread and pull it through both loops. The bead will be caught within the single crochet, facing away from you.

increasing and decreasing

Let's examine the top of the single crochet stitch. After you crochet into a loop and complete the stitch, it will lay flat against the top of the round in a sort of "teardrop" shape. If you look at these photos and the accompanying figure, you'll see the difference between the front half of the stitch, the back half of the stitch, and the whole stitch. Unless otherwise directed, you should always crochet into the whole stitch to create the designs in this book.

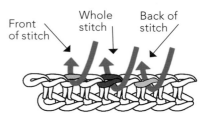

Front

Whole

Back

Some of the design patterns will call for increases of one stitch in certain rounds. To do this, you'll simply crochet two stitches in the same space. In hex bases, you'll increase six times in every round.

To decrease by one stitch, pull up the loop as if you were going to make a single crochet. Don't wrap the thread around the hook yet. Instead, insert the hook in the next stitch, and pull up another loop, so there are three loops on the hook. Now bring your bead down the thread and wrap the thread around the hook. Pull through all three loops to complete the decrease.

A series of increases, shown in a hex base design

Pull up one loop as for regular single crochet. (Don't wrap the thread)

Insert the hook in the next stitch

Pull up another loop to have three loops on the hook

Wrap the thread around the hook

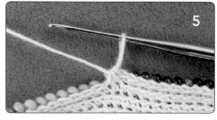

Pull through all three loops to complete the decrease

18

working in the round and stepping up

Most of the designs you'll create in this book will be worked in the round, with the inside of the work facing you, and the beaded side facing away from you. The result is really a tube, though it may appear flat when you use it. This is different from a circular hex base, which we'll examine later.

You'll notice that working in the round, done properly, produces very little distortion. The beads will square up to each other nicely, eliminating the need for steam shaping or wet blocking (page 20).

In preparation for the start of each new round, you'll "step up." It's important for you to master this technique, as the success of your project-in-the-round will depend on it.

When you've completed the last single crochet in the round, join that stitch to the first single crochet of that round, using a slip stitch. Remember to be careful about your tension. Now make one chain.

When you make the first single crochet of the new round, you'll insert the hook into the same space as the slip stitch you just made; this will always be the top of the first single crochet in the previous round.

After joining with a slip stitch, chain one

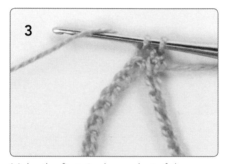

Insert the hook in the same space as the slip stitch

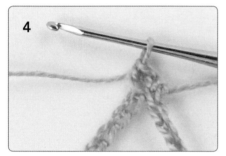

Make the first single crochet of the new round. Pull up a loop and wrap the thread

Pull through both loops to complete the first single crochet of the new round

You can position your step-up at the side seam in a flat design; this produces a very clean look in the finished piece. For a design that's built on a hex base, which we'll examine in Chapter 3, the step-up is easily made at the same location as the step-up in the hex itself.

For gusseted designs, I like to position the step-up in the center of the gusset itself. You can step up at any corner, but sometimes you'll want to use a decorative motif in the corner, which will make the step-up a bit confusing.

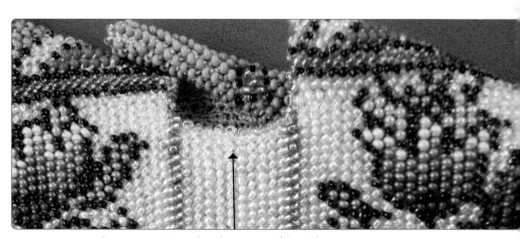

Step-up positioned at the center of the side gusset

adding a thread

To add a thread, pull up a loop in the desired position, chain one, then single crochet—with or without a bead, according to your design—in the same space as the loop. To secure the thread, crochet right over the tail for two or three stitches.

working back and forth

In some of the projects, you'll need to work back and forth instead of in the round. This may seem a bit daunting to you at first, but with practice it will start to feel more natural. I don't use this technique as often as working in the round, because the resulting crochet fabric has a tendency to be slightly distorted. You can correct this distortion with wet block or steam stretching.

This technique is very useful for making flaps, and for stitching sections where a bag will be attached to a handle. When working back and forth, you'll need to pay special attention to your threading. Designs in this book in which you'll work back and forth are marked with arrows to indicate the correct threading direction for each row, as shown in the sample stitching diagram here.

A handle attachment section worked back and forth

Rows marked with arrows to indicate threading direction

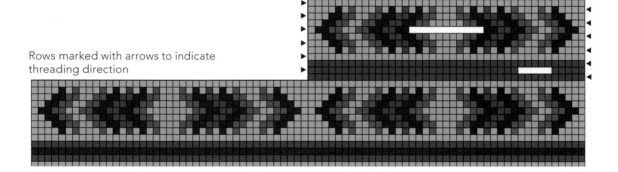

blocking and stretching

To wet block, saturate the piece in water, then roll it in a towel to draw out all the excess water. Stretch the piece into the correct shape, and—using rust-resistant pins—pin it to the surface of your ironing board. Allow the piece to dry completely before unpinning it.

A simpler method is steam stretching. Place the piece on your ironing board and cover it with a dish towel or other thin protective fabric. Using a steam iron, infuse the crochet with steam, then stretch it to the correct shape before it cools. Use extreme caution! Beads are made of glass and therefore retain heat, so wear gloves or some kind of hand protection while handling the piece. Under no circumstances should you place the hot surface of the iron directly onto the glass beads.

When you're working back and forth, you'll reverse direction at the end of each row, instead of stepping up. When the row is complete, chain one, then turn the work around so the beads are facing you. Now insert the hook into the top of the last single crochet of the previous round, but insert it from back to front. Position your thread at the front of the work, then bring a bead down the thread. Position the bead very close to the hook and the loops. Now wrap the thread under the hook; pull up a loop so there are two loops on the hook, and the bead is caught in the stitch. Wrap the thread around the hook back to front, and pull through both loops to complete the stitch. The bead should be on the same side as the beads of the previous rows or rounds.

Insert the hook backwards through the whole top of the stitch

Pull up a loop and chain one (first stitch of the row only)

Bring a bead down the thread and wrap under the hook

Pull through to make two loops on the hook

Wrap thread over the hook from back to front

Pull through both loops to complete the backward stitch

In all subsequent backward stitches, insert the hook into the next stitch, back to front; bring the bead down the thread and wrap under the hook; pull up a loop; wrap the thread over the hook back to front, and pull through both loops to complete the backward stitch (see the photo at right).

At the end of the backward row, turn the work so the unbeaded side is facing you. Chain one, make a "normal" single crochet in the last stitch of the previous row, and work normally across that row.

Chapter 3

techniques

Some of the techniques in the chapter—such as threading beads—will be essential for all the projects that follow. Others will be necessary only if you're making a project with a hem, or a rectangular or hex base. Either way, you're likely to refer back to this resource section often.

threading

Bead crochet is unlike nonbeaded crochet, in that you'll have to do some advance work in the projects you'll be making. You first need to thread the beads onto the fiber. When you look at some of the larger pieces, you'll probably realize without being told that the threading needs to be done in sections. And before we move on, here's one of the most important concepts in tapestry bead crochet:

The last bead threaded in a section will be the first bead crocheted, and the first bead threaded will be the last bead crocheted.

Because the pieces made here will grow from the bottom up, the first section you do is the bottom section, and then you'll work upward. You can see the progression as a piece is built in illustrations A through D.

The patterns for the designs are charted, much as counted cross-stitch would be. You'll crochet in horizontal rows, so your threading should also be in horizontal rows. I always thread my beads from right to left because I'm right-handed. If I were left-handed, I'd probably thread my beads onto the fiber from left to right. Images with lettering or numerals should be threaded in mirror image, but in most cases it really doesn't matter how the design is positioned. Most designs will look equally good facing in either direction. Take a look here at the two sides of the Phoenix Carryall (page 32), for example, and you'll see that the bird looks just fine facing either way.

A

B

C

D

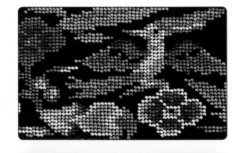

Your threading direction must be consistent throughout the entire piece. I usually thread on seven to ten rows at a time, depending on the width of the rows. If the rows are very long—say, 100 beads or more—I may only thread on three or four rows at a time. You'll discover your comfort zone with experience.

To begin, start at the top row of the section (remember, the first bead threaded is the last bead crocheted) and add rows from the top to the bottom of the section. In the case of a bag with two sides, you'll be threading your design chart twice, for a front and a back, unless the specific directions for a design tell you to thread two different designs.

keeping track of rounds

We've been talking about "rows" up to now, but what we're really doing, in most cases, is "rounds." At the start of each round, you'll step up with a precise set of stitches; this important process is discussed in the section on page 19. You have to be able to identify the end of one row or round and the start of the next, so you'll know where to step up. It's also important to determine if your round has been threaded and crocheted correctly; if you have no beads left at the step up, chances are good that your threading and stitching are both correct. You need to incorporate the identifier into your threading.

This is easily done if you use paper markers. Take an old newspaper and trim off an unprinted strip, no more than ⅓ inch (8 mm) wide (photo 1), and cut it into little squares (photo 2). You'll start your threading at the top of a section, and work in your chosen direction across the row. At the end of the row, run the needle through the center of the paper square and carry it down the thread along with your beads (photo 3). As you crochet, you'll simply tear off the paper when you reach the end of the round.

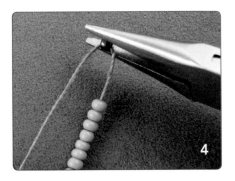

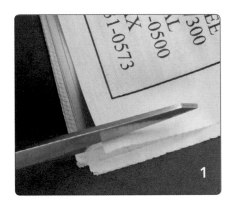

fixing mistakes

You have a few different ways to deal with errors. If you realize your mistake with only a few beads threaded on after it, just remove the beads back to the last correct point, and then rethread. If you have one too many beads, you can crush out the extra bead with your handy little pliers (photo 4). (Always wear eye protection.) If you've skipped a bead, tie a snippet of thread around your crochet thread at the error point; when you reach that point in the row, crochet right through the stitch without a bead, and sew a bead in place later (photo 5).

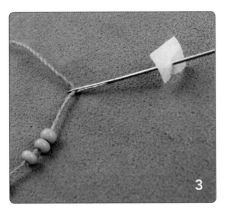

basic tubular bead crochet

Though the primary topic of this book is tapestry bead crochet, you'll need tubular bead crochet for some of the projects. You may already be familiar with this technique; if not, we'll take a look at it now.

To begin your tubular bead crochet, you'll need to refer to the directions of the specific design for the threading pattern and number of repeats needed. After threading on the beads, make a slip knot, as you would to start any chain.

Make six chains, each one with a bead. To chain with a bead, slide a bead down the thread until it hangs below the hook. Wrap the thread around the hook and pull it through the loop.

Each stitch you make after the initial chain is complete will consist of five distinct steps: IN, OVER, DOWN, AROUND, and THROUGH.

Step 1: IN

Insert the hook into the first beaded chain. Don't pierce the thread with your hook or put the hook through the hole in the bead (figure 1).

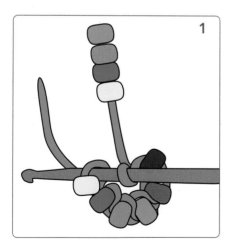

Step 2: OVER

Push the bead over to the far side of the hook. This is an important step; in order for the whole process to be successful, all the beads must "land" on the outside of the tube. The thread that carries your beads must be positioned to the right of the bead that has been passed over the hook, as in figure 2.

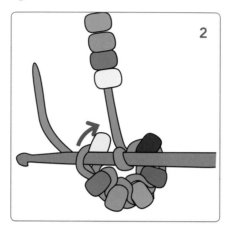

Step 3: DOWN

Bring a bead down the thread as shown. The thread must be positioned to the right of the bead that has been passed over the hook in step 2. If it's not positioned to the right, the bead will end up on the inside of the tube when the stitch is completed.

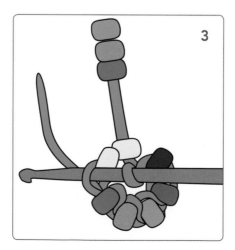

Step 4: AROUND

Wrap the thread around the hook from back to front (toward yourself) so the new bead and the bead that has been passed over the hook are touching. The new thread will cross over the loop that's on the hook.

Step 5: THROUGH

You now have two loops on the hook, and the thread is wrapped around the hook. Pull the wrapped thread through both loops. *Note:* You can pull the wrapped thread through one loop at a time, using two motions to complete this step, until you're comfortable pulling the wrapped thread through both loops.

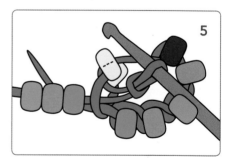

This completes the stitch. Repeat the five numbered steps until you have six completed stitches. The photo at right shows the tube as you progress.

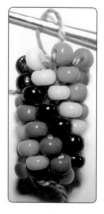

invisible tube joining

Sometimes you'll need to join your tube of crochet into a continuous ring. The technique for doing this is shown in the following three steps with diagrams.

One important note: You must finish your tube with the last bead in the pattern repeat. You need to do this so that when you join to the start of the tube, the beads remain "in pattern." In the diagrams here, the blue beads indicate the last round crocheted, and the beige beads indicate the first round crocheted.

Step 1

If you are working in a pattern, make sure that the beginning and end of the tube you wish to join invisibly are "in pattern" with each other. In other words, if you continued to crochet from the end round using the beads of the first round, the pattern would be correct. When you're satisfied this is true, cut the end thread (shown in red), leaving a tail about 12 inches (30.5 cm) long, then bind by running the cut end through the last loop on your hook. Put a needle on the starting thread tail and bury it within the tube itself by running the needle into and then through the fibers of the tube. Take care not to run the tail thread through the center holes of the beads themselves, or the tube will be distorted.

Put the end thread tail (red) onto a needle and bring it out of the hole of the last bead you crocheted into. Align the end and start of the tube as shown in figure 1.

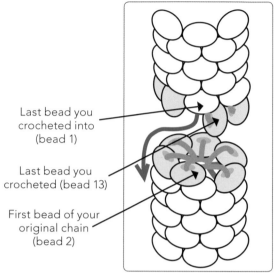

Last bead you crocheted into (bead 1)

Last bead you crocheted (bead 13)

First bead of your original chain (bead 2)

1

Step 2

Follow the thread path shown in figure 2. The dark blue dots indicate the thread that holds each bead in place on the tube. The thread must go in this specific path for the joint to appear seamless.

Step 3

As you progress, draw the tube ends close together and take out the slack in the thread. When you do this, you will notice (see figure 3, bead #3) that the beads of the end round (blue) will shift into the horizontal position, and thus appear to be attached to the beads of the beginning round (beige). Continue around the tube until the two ends are firmly joined in proper alignment. You may want to continue sewing through beads to secure the joint even further; you could even make another complete round. Secure the excess thread within the weave, taking care to run the thread only through the fibers and not through the bead holes. When you're certain the thread is secure, trim off the excess, taking care not to cut any of the threads that hold beads.

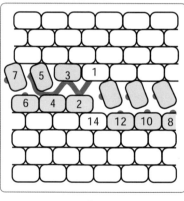

3

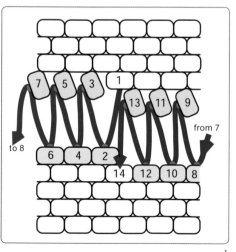

2

adding hems

Depending on what your bead crochet project will be used for, you may want to add a hem on an open end. A small hem stabilizes the opening and creates a finished, professional look.

Here's how to add one. Using your crochet fiber, simply add three or four rounds of unbeaded single crochet. Leave a very long thread tail, perhaps a yard (0.9 m) or more. Secure the thread by pulling it through the last loop.

Now use invisible stitches and a sharp-pointed needle to secure the hem flat against the inside of the crochet. You don't need more than eight stitches per inch (2.5 cm). Don't pull the thread too tightly or the hem will pucker; pull it gently until the hem rests against the back of the crochet. When the hem is complete, secure the thread end invisibly within the crochet and trim it.

Make three or four rows of unbeaded single crochet

Start stitching near the step-up point

Make small invisible stitches using the same thread

closing an open end

In some cases, your starting end will be closed, especially if you're working on a shaped item or a project that starts with a hex or rectangle base. If you're doing a simple tube such as a music player holder or an eyeglass case, however, you'll have two open ends. You'll probably hem the top of the case, and you'll need to close the open end.

You'll get the best result, as with hemming, if you use the crochet thread to close the opening. It's nearly impossible to achieve a perfectly neat starting end, so we'll accommodate for this in closing the end. It's a good idea to press the open end before starting; this tames unruly stitches and makes them easier to handle.

Hold the edge closed between your fingertips, and use a back-and-forth motion through the end row to join the edges together. Your crochet thread will be invisible. Make your stitches less than ¼ inch (6 mm) apart for stability, and work back across the opening in the opposite direction for added security. When the end is well closed, weave the thread into the crochet and trim it.

making a rectangular base

An important part of the construction of a three-dimensional piece with gussets and corners is the rectangular base. We touched briefly on this in the section on working back and forth on page 20. Designs worked in the round with side gussets are usually started with a rectangular base; this takes the place of the starting chain in a flat design worked in the round. You'll build your first round of the design area on the outer edges of the rectangular base. Illustrations A and B show an overview of how the sides of a rectangular design are built from a flat rectangular base.

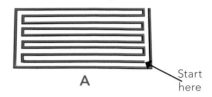

A

Start here

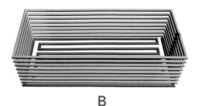

B

Illustration C shows the direction of the stitching, starting at the inside right lower corner. The rose-colored symbols show the corner turns in the creation of the rectangular base.

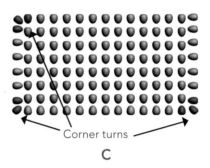

Corner turns

C

The rectangle itself is started with a chain. For the projects in this book with a rectangular base, the directions will indicate the number of chains required. If you're designing your own, you'll start with a chain that has *one fewer* than the number of stitches in the bottom row of the design area.

You'll work in back-and-forth rows. The number of back-and-forth rows you stitch will be one fewer than the width of the gusset. Refer to illustration D as you follow these steps:

Step 1

Build rows one on top of the last, turning at the ends of the rows, until you have one fewer than the desired number of rows for the width of the gusset.

Step 2

In the last stitch of the last row, work three single crochet with beads, thereby creating a squared corner.

Step 3

Now work down the side, placing one single crochet with a bead in the end stitch of each row but the last. In that end stitch, work three single crochet with beads, creating a second squared corner.

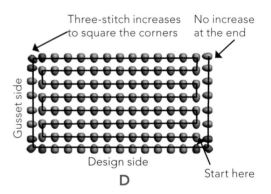

Three-stitch increases to square the corners

No increase at the end

Gusset side

Design side

Start here

D

Step 4

Work across the bottom in the other side of the original chain, placing one single crochet with a bead in each stitch, except the last, in which you'll again make three single crochet with beads.

Step 5

Work up the opposite side, again placing one stitch in the end of each row. Make only one single crochet with a bead in the last stitch.

Step 6

The design side of the rectangular base has the same number of stitches as the base row of the design, as shown in illustration E.

E

making a hex base

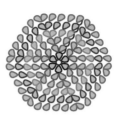

The rounded designs in this book are all built on a hex base. As the name implies, this is a geometric stitching pattern based on six repeats. Because the thread is very flexible, the hex morphs into a circular shape. If you're working in only one color, follow the project directions for the number of rounds and the color of the beads to be used. If there's a pattern involved, you'll follow a charted design like the one at right.

Hex bases are begun with an unbeaded chain of six (photo 1). You'll join this chain into a ring with a slip stitch (photo 2 and 3). Make one chain (photo 4), then make six single crochet with beads in the ring (photo 5). As you make these single crochet, catch the tail thread in the stitch, making sure not to split the tail thread with your hook (photo 6). You'll use this encased thread later like a cinch to neaten the center of the hex. Join the round, and step up.

Now make only one single crochet with bead in the same space (the first stitch in the previous round). Make two in the second stitch. You've now increased two stitches to three. Make one single crochet in the next, and two in the stitch after that. Repeat this one-two pattern all around, then join the round.

Now you'll step up, as you will at the start of every new round. The step-up in the hex base is the same as in a flat piece. Join the last single crochet to the first with a slip stitch. Start the round by making one single crochet with a bead in the same space as the slip stitch. Now you'll make another single crochet with a bead in the same space, increasing one stitch to two. Make two single crochet with beads in the remaining five single crochet of the round (photo 7).

Step up again; make one single crochet with a bead in the first stitch, then two single crochet with bead in the next. Notice how all the increases in the hex rounds will take place in the second stitch of the increase in the previous round.

Now you'll make use of that encased tail thread. Photo 9 shows how the outside will look before you tighten the tail thread. Photo 10 shows how the outside looks after the thread is tightened. As you can see, it makes quite a difference in the appearance.

1

Chain six

2

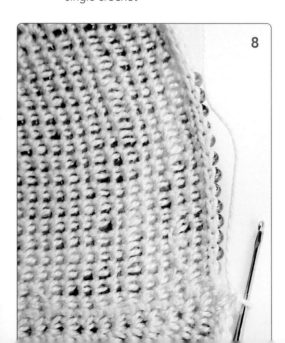

3

Join with a slip stitch

4

Chain one

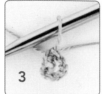

5

Make six single crochet in the ring

6

Catch the initial tail thread in the single crochet

7

8

9

Tail thread unpulled

10

Tail thread pulled

The edge of the hex will tend to curl over toward the back, especially if your tension is tight or if your beads are on the large side. You can easily correct this by pressing (see Blocking and Stretching, page 20). The hex can be used to create a small bag, as in the Chatelaine shown below left. But in many cases you'll build walls upward from the outer round of the hex, as shown here with the bottom of the Lotus Purse (below right). Your wall pattern should have the same number of stitches as the outermost round of the base.

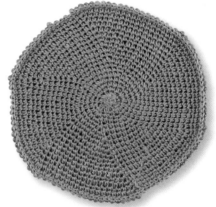

Unpressed

Pressed

Chapter 4

basic patterns

These are the patterns that will get you started. Don't be fooled by the rich designs—there are no tricks to these treasures!

phoenix carryall

ring quartet

sunflower
& feathers case

listen up! pouch

castle tapestry bag

a peach of a bag

aztec & bargello case

leather bargello bag

spectacle case

A dynamic design that's simple to make, this Phoenix bag is a great beginner project.
Beyond the basic crochet, you'll learn how to insert a zipper closure with fabric lining.

phoenix carryall

phoenix carryall

before you begin

It's so simple to create an envelope bag. You just thread on your pattern, repeating each row twice, then crochet in the round, with your step-up at the side seam. In the Phoenix pattern, you'll use two colors of thread: butter yellow in the geometric strips at the top and bottom of the piece and navy blue in the central design area. Notice how the bright gold bead color changes when used on the different colors of thread.

what you need

beads (for two sides)

Czech #BL605 11°,
matte bright gold AB (806 beads)

Miyuki #2028 11°,
matte seafoam (570 beads)

Czech #73030M 11°,
matte dusty rose (668 beads)

Czech #24020M 11°,
matte opaque light amethyst
AB (704 beads)

Toho #8DF 11°,
matte navy (2,230 beads)

Czech #93510 11°,
opaque persimmon (240 beads)

Czech #93170 11°,
opaque bright red (244 beads)

Toho #176F 11°,
matte pale gray AB (170 beads)

Czech #23020 11°,
opaque medium amethyst
(306 beads)

Czech #06013 11°,
opaque buttercream (1,828
beads)

additional materials and tools

#12 perle cotton, butter yellow, 5 g

#12 perle cotton, navy blue, 15 g

7-inch (17.8 cm) light-duty zipper,
light yellow

Coordinating color of sewing
thread for zipper

Lightweight satin fabric for lining, approximately 8 x 10 inches (20.3 x 25.4 cm)

Crochet hooks, beading needles,
and scissors

Sewing needle

Fabric glue

what you do

1 Review the Getting Started section on page 15 (and the sections on basic stitches that follow it) and the Threading section on page 22. Then see the stitch chart on page 35. The initial chain for this design is 142. It's best to load all seven rounds of the bottom yellow section to start, then add the dark blue area in five or six sections.

2 Add the top yellow section in one loading as well. The stitch chart will indicate where to change thread colors.

3 Secure any loose threads within the crochet and trim. Place the piece bead-side down on a thick towel and infuse the fibers with steam from your iron. Stretch to correct any distortion and maintain the position until the fibers are cool. Note that glass beads will retain heat for several minutes. Use the sewing needle to sew the bottom edges together using your crochet thread tail (photo 1).

phoenix carryall

4 With the slide at the clamped end, trim off the zipper so it's about ½ inch (1.3 cm) longer than the width of the bag (photo 2).

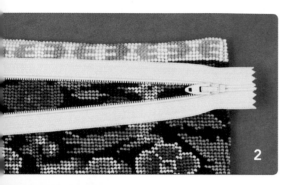

5 Using sewing thread, make stopper stitches on the cut end of the zipper (photo 3). Trim the excess coils off the end of the zipper outside the stopper threads, and tuck the ends under. Secure them with a few stitches (these won't show). A small dot of glue will prevent fraying on the cut ends.

6 Sew the zipper in place so the edge of the beading is within ¹/₈ inch (3 mm) of the zipper coils (photo 4). Baste it with large stitches first, then sew on the front surface, catching only the top surface of the zipper fabric. Don't run the sewing thread through any beads.

7 Fold your lining fabric in half with the wrong sides together. Place the bag on the lining fabric so the seamed bottom is aligned with the fold on the fabric. Use the bag as a guide to cut the lining about ½ inch (1.3 cm) larger at the top and on both sides (photo 5).

8 Sew the side seams so the lining will fit inside the bag (photo 6).

9 Notch the bottom corners and press the seams so they lie flat against the lining (photo 7). Press the top edges of the lining so the edge will be more than ¹/₈ inch (3 mm) away from the zipper coils; if it's closer, it may catch in the zipper. You may need to try the fit and make some adjustments.

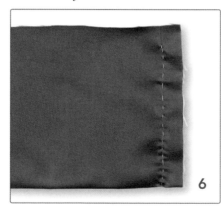

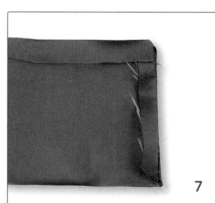

10 Turn the lining inside out and position it within the bag. Secure the lining in place with tiny stitches along the top edge (photo 8).

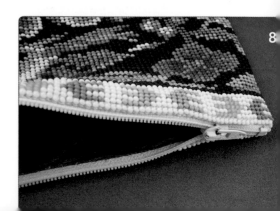

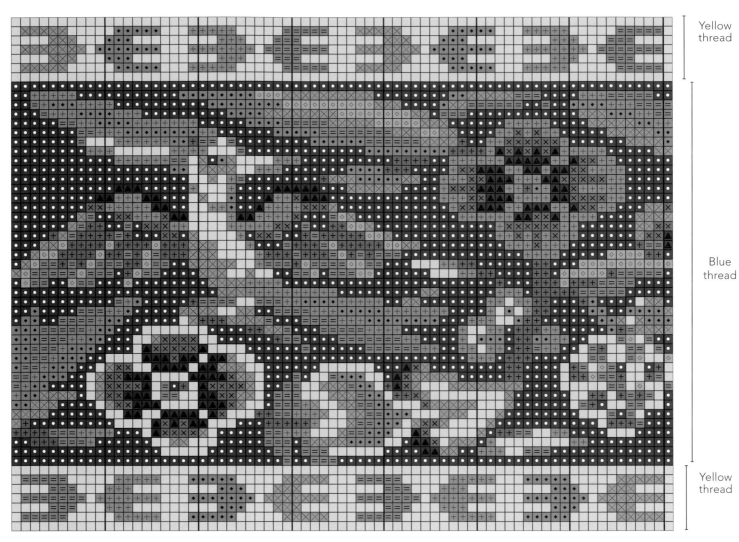

Yellow thread

Blue thread

Yellow thread

KEY

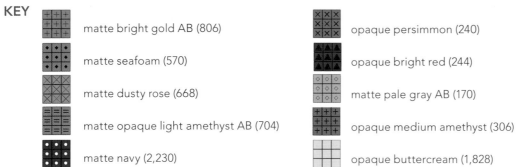

matte bright gold AB (806)

matte seafoam (570)

matte dusty rose (668)

matte opaque light amethyst AB (704)

matte navy (2,230)

opaque persimmon (240)

opaque bright red (244)

matte pale gray AB (170)

opaque medium amethyst (306)

opaque buttercream (1,828)

These elegant napkin rings are great learning pieces. They're easy to thread, and you can tell almost immediately if you've made a mistake, because the patterns are geometric and predictable.

ring
quartet

ring quartet

before you begin

These rings are stitched with your choice of one color of seed beads and one color of Japanese drop beads, so you can easily coordinate them with any dinnerware pattern. The colors in the example shown—just in case they already go perfectly with your cloth napkins—are matte opaque aqua for the 11° beads and matte transparent teal for the Japanese drops. Starting these pieces is easy because you'll work three rounds of unbeaded crochet before stitching with beads, which gives you something to hang on to. And they're so simple to finish—just a three-row hem on both sides.

what you need

beads (for two sides)

Two varieties in the colors of your choice:

Czech 11° seed beads

Japanese drop beads, 3 to 4 mm

(The bead counts for each pattern are indicated next to the stitch charts on page 38.)

additional materials and tools

#12 perle cotton in a color complementary to the 11° seed beads, 3 g per napkin ring

Crochet hooks, beading needles, and scissors

what you do

1 It's helpful to put the beads in two separate piles, and then take from each pile according to the threading chart. Gather your materials to follow one of the threading charts on page 38. If you haven't already done so, wind the thread onto a winding card (see page 14 for a template) before threading. Thread the needle and begin your threading. (Review the Getting Started section on page 15 and the Threading section on page 22 if necessary.)

2 Because they're small, you can thread each ring on in two sections or even just one. The initial chain on each ring is 60. Leave a thread tail of 6 inches (15.2 cm) for later use in finishing.

3 For each pattern, crochet three unbeaded rounds to start, then begin the beaded crochet. Work until the beads are gone, then add three more rounds of unbeaded crochet. Use the unbeaded sections as hems on both sides of the ring. Cut the thread 6 inches (15.2 cm) away from the last loop and pull it through the last loop to secure it. You'll use this thread for sewing the hem in place.

ring quartet

4 To finish the rings, simply turn the three-round unbeaded sections inside the rings, and secure them in place with invisible stitches using the 6-inch (15.2 cm) tail threads on both sides.

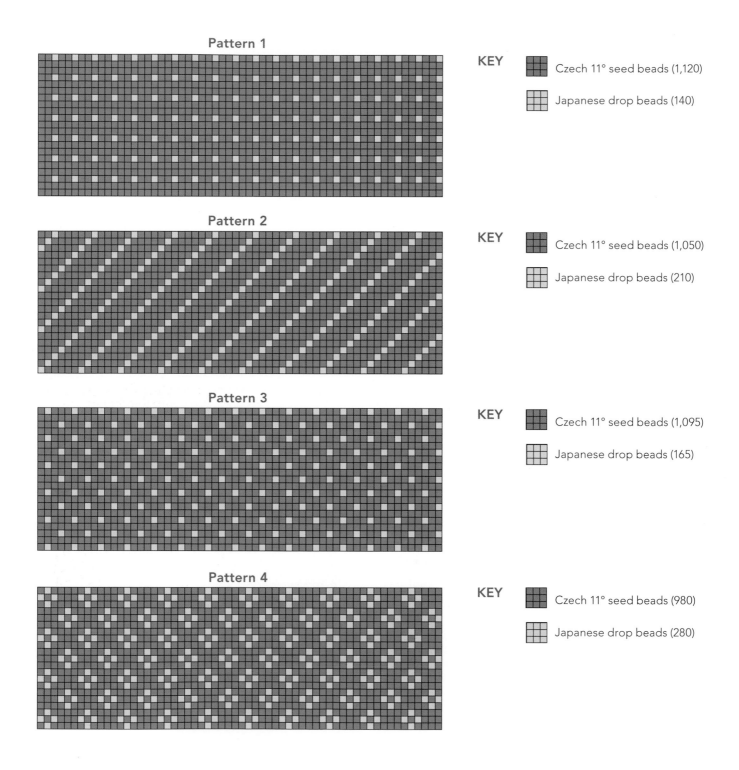

Pattern 1

KEY
Czech 11° seed beads (1,120)
Japanese drop beads (140)

Pattern 2

KEY
Czech 11° seed beads (1,050)
Japanese drop beads (210)

Pattern 3

KEY
Czech 11° seed beads (1,095)
Japanese drop beads (165)

Pattern 4

KEY
Czech 11° seed beads (980)
Japanese drop beads (280)

sunflower & feathers case

Sunflowers and feathers seem such a natural pair; think of the beautiful yellow finches that perch on the big, lush blossoms and steal the seeds— summer at its glorious best.

sunflower & feathers case

before you begin

This project is a simple flat case, with absolutely no finishing required. Just crochet and go! It's perfectly sized for a small cell phone or personal music player, as well as glasses. The stitching here is also a wonderful example of how the color of the thread can have a noticeable and positive effect on the look of the beads.

what you need

beads

All Czech 11° beads:

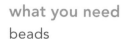 #BL558 silk pale yellow (2,295 beads)

 #83130 opaque medium yellow (318 beads)

 #93110 opaque orange-gold (159 beads)

 #BL466 matte topaz AB (449 beads)

 #01710 silk light copper (176 beads)

 #13600 opaque rust (239 beads)

 #13780 opaque dark brown (221 beads)

 #23980 black (585 beads)

 #63000 opaque light blue (1,058 beads)

 #63050 opaque medium blue (954 beads)

 #25843 silk pale lime (181 beads)

 #53410 opaque light green (179 beads)

 #53430 opaque olive green (89 beads)

 #25511 silk pine green (99 beads)

 #57102 Ceylon white (165 beads)

additional materials and tools

#12 perle cotton, bright gold, about 10 g

Crochet hooks, beading needles, and scissors

Sewing needle

what you do

1 Following the instructions for threading on page 22, thread on the bottom of the design shown on the stitch chart at right.

2 As you start your initial chain of 82, leave about 8 inches (20.3 cm) as a starting tail thread. Working from bottom to top, crochet the rows in the stitch chart.

3 Crochet an additional four rounds at the top of the case to use as the hem. Roll the hem under the beaded crochet and stitch it in place with the remaining tail thread, or add a new perle cotton thread.

4 Following the instructions in the Closing an Open End section (page 26), use the starting tail thread or a new perle cotton thread to sew the bottom seam of the case closed.

tip

For more design fun, you can add a button and loop at the top as a closure. Put these in place after you stitch the hem.

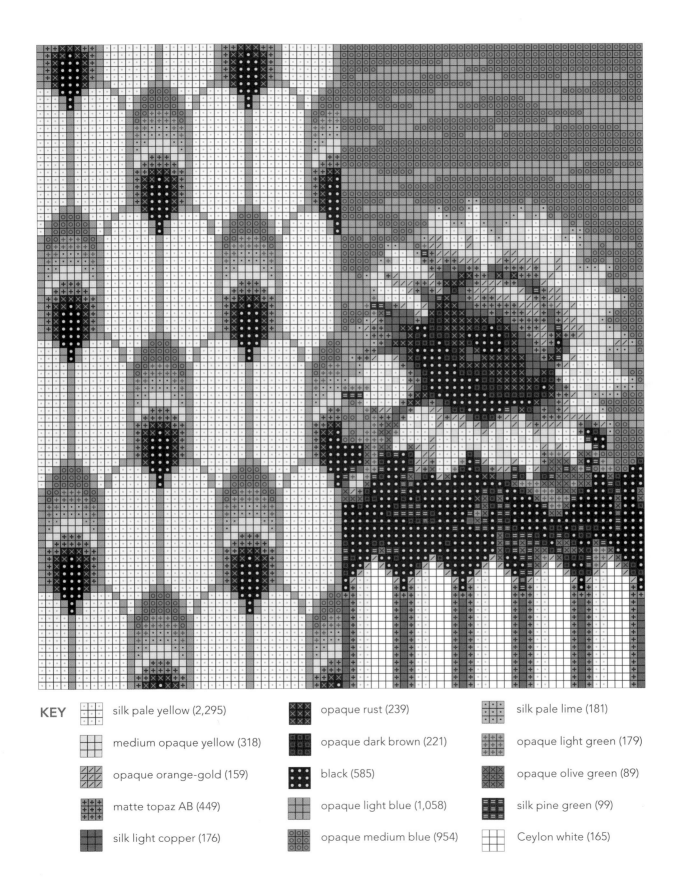

KEY

silk pale yellow (2,295)	
medium opaque yellow (318)	
opaque orange-gold (159)	
matte topaz AB (449)	
silk light copper (176)	
opaque rust (239)	
opaque dark brown (221)	
black (585)	
opaque light blue (1,058)	
opaque medium blue (954)	
silk pale lime (181)	
opaque light green (179)	
opaque olive green (89)	
silk pine green (99)	
Ceylon white (165)	

An ordinary cell phone or portable music player
instantly becomes a smart accessory
once it has a home in this classic design.

listen up!
pouch

listen up! pouch

before you begin

After making this fabulous bead design created by Lauren Miller, you can use the blank pattern on page 127 to come up with your own. You'll use two important techniques here: creating a buttonhole and an opening for the headphone jack, and stitching back-and-forth rows.

what you need

beads

 Miyuki #648 11°, light blue alabaster (1,666 beads)

 Czech #60014 11°, dark blue (1,118 beads)

 Toho #222 11°, dark copper (1,105 beads))

 Toho #223 11°, light bronze (1,076 beads)

 Toho #557F 11°, matte galvanized gold (840 beads)

additional materials and tools

#12 perle cotton, medium blue

Button with shank, ¾ inch (1.9 cm) in diameter

Sewing thread in a complementary color

Crochet hooks, beading needles, and scissors

what you do

1 Thread on and stitch the piece as charted on page 44 (starting at the bottom), switching to back-and-forth stitching in the flap area at the top. For the back-and-forth section, thread beads onto the thread in the order of the direction of the arrows, as in the illustration below. Place a paper marker at the end of each row as described on page 23. The blank areas in the chart will form the buttonhole and the hole to allow access to the headphone jack.

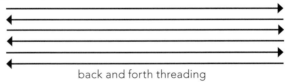
back and forth threading

2 When all the crochet is complete, stitch an additional four unbeaded rows, also back and forth, which will serve as the flap hem.

3 Attach a thread in the outermost edge of the top row of the front of the case (shown in the left half of the stitching chart). Stitch four back-and-forth unbeaded rows that will serve as the hem for the front inside of the case, as shown in photo 1.

listen up! pouch

4 When the front inside hem is complete, stitch the button in place with ordinary sewing thread of a coordinating color, making several passes of thread for security. Make sure to position the button so the shank lands in the center of the buttonhole (see photo 2). Make the button hole using the technique described on page 74.

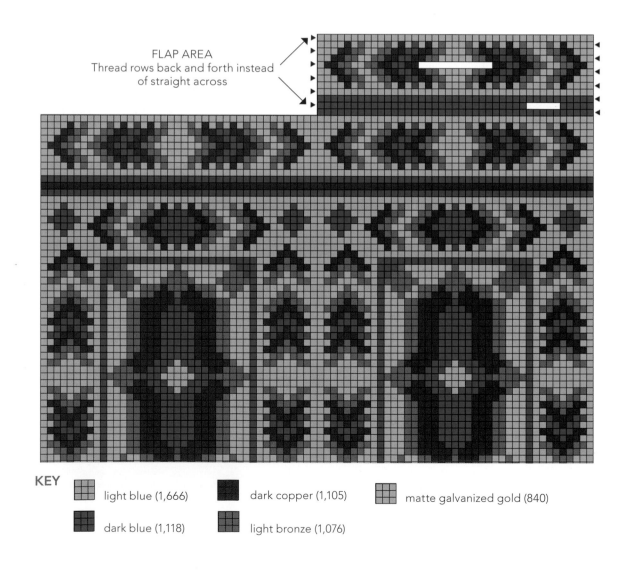

FLAP AREA
Thread rows back and forth instead
of straight across

KEY

light blue (1,666) dark copper (1,105) matte galvanized gold (840)

dark blue (1,118) light bronze (1,076)

castle
tapestry
bag

This exquisite bag doesn't just depict a castle.
It also evokes one of those gorgeous and historic
tapestries you might see on the *inside* of one.

castle tapestry bag

before you begin

Despite its complex appearance, this flat envelope bag is actually quite easy to create. Because the rows in this project are long (142 stitches in a complete round), you'll find it best to thread on no more than six or seven rounds at a time.

what you need

beads for both sides together

Czech 11° beads
(unless otherwise noted):

#10020M matte light topaz
(55 beads)

#BL650 matte medium topaz
(155 beads)

#10090M matte deep topaz
(222 beads)

#37132 pale Ceylon blue
(1,341 beads)

#64020 lustered light blue
(659 beads)

#68050 lustered medium blue
(1,214 beads)

#23220 silk light orchid
(58 beads)

#38020 lustered medium
periwinkle (624 beads)

#38040 lustered sapphire blue
(1,290 beads)

#23720 silk light rose
(504 beads)

#23940 silk medium rose
(473 beads)

#BL569 silk deep rose
(189 beads)

#03152 opaque pale olive
(634 beads)

#53410 opaque lime
(591 beads)

#53210 opaque bright grass
green (305 beads)

#53240 opaque teal green
(255 beads)

#23560 silk light khaki
(202 beads)

Toho #513F 11°, matte light olive
(169 beads)

#13600 opaque rust
(334 beads)

#13780 opaque dark brown
(269 beads)

#23980 opaque black
(158 beads)

additional materials and tools

#12 perle cotton, beige or eggshell,
10 g

For the handle and netted fringe:

Czech #48102 11° lustered transparent crystal seed beads (1,485 plus up to 100 more to lengthen the handle)

80 round white natural freshwater pearls, 4 or 5 mm (plus up to 20 more to lengthen the handle)

8 rice-shaped white natural freshwater pearls, 8 x 10 mm

1 round white pearl, 12 mm
(a Swarovski pearl may be used)

Nylon beading thread in a neutral color

Crochet hooks, beading needles, and scissors

what you do

crochet the bag

1 The front and back of the bag are crocheted together at the same time, working from the bottom and arranged as shown on pages 48 and 49. The two charts are the same number of units high and wide (71 x 71). The initial chain is 142 stitches. Leave a thread tail of about 12 inches (30.5 cm), which you'll use later in seaming the bottom edge.

2 When the crochet is complete, add a three-round hem at the top edge. Stitch the bottom edge together, using the 12-inch (30.5 cm) tail of perle cotton you left in the initial threading.

make the netted fringe

3 To make the netted fringe (photo 1), first cut a 60-inch (1.5 m) length of beading nylon and attach it to the bottom right corner of the crochet. Secure the thread by weaving back and forth a few times.

4 Pick up 11 Czech 11° lustered transparent crystal beads; run the thread through the bottom seam just below the fourth bead from the right of the bottom row.

5 Run back through the last bead and pick up 10 of the same bead. Run the thread through the bottom seam just below the fourth bead away.

6 Continue across the bottom seam, picking up 10 beads and skipping three beads on the bottom row. You'll loop into the bottom seam every fourth bead all along the bottom edge until there are 17 loops. For the 18th and last loop, pick up 10 beads again, then loop into the left corner. Run back through the last five beads. This is shown in the Netted Fringe diagram (below) as a red thread path.

1

netted fringe

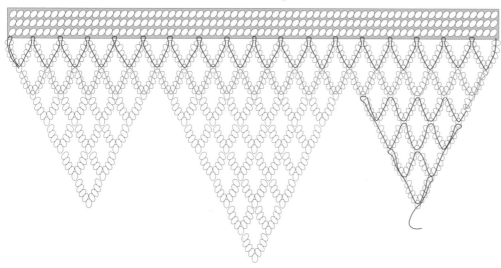

7 Pick up nine beads and run through the center bead of the next loop. Repeat this across the row, as shown by the green thread path. When you reach the last loop, run back through the last five beads added.

8 Make the right peak of the net as shown with the blue thread path. This same thread path will be used to make the center and left peaks as well.

9 If you need additional thread, attach the new thread within the bottom seam of the crochet and weave through the netting by the shortest route to reach the continuation point.

castle tapestry bag

back of bag

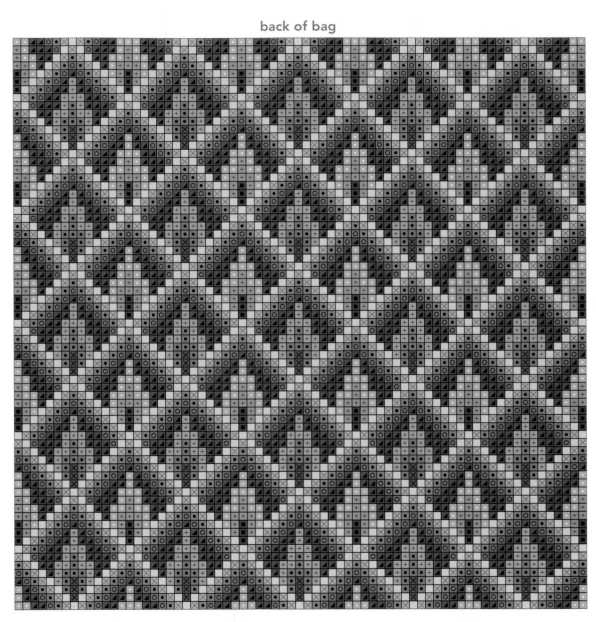

KEY
front
and
back

matte light topaz (55)

matte medium topaz (155)

matte deep topaz (222)

pale Ceylon blue (1,341)

lustered light blue (659)

lustered medium blue (1,214)

silk light orchid (58)

lustered medium periwinkle (624)

lustered sapphire blue (1,290)

silk light rose (504)

silk medium rose (473)

silk deep rose (189)

front of bag

KEY
front
and
back

opaque pale olive (634)

opaque lime (591)

opaque bright grass green (305)

opaque teal green (255)

silk light khaki (202)

matte light olive (169)

opaque rust (334)

opaque dark brown (269)

opaque black (158)

castle tapestry bag

make the handle with netting

10 After you've added the netting to the bottom of the bag, add one row of loops all around the top edge in the same manner as for the bottom netting. Following the Handle with Netting diagram (below) for the handle, add the two peaks as diagrammed, again in the same manner as the peaks were made for the bottom netting. Secure the thread when the peaks are complete. You can make handles on both the front and the back (see photo bottom right) or on one side only.

11 Using a new thread, string the round 4- to 5-mm freshwater pearls with three Czech 11° lustered transparent crystal beads in between each pearl. Continue until you've reached the length of handle you'd like. A length of 12 to 14 inches (30.5 to 35.6 cm) is good. Add one 11° crystal bead after the last pearl, then add one larger, rice-shaped pearl. Run through the top bead of one peak.

12 Run back through all the handle beads; add one 11° crystal bead after the last small pearl, and one large pearl; run through the top bead of the opposite peak. Run back through all the beads and pearls, and then through the peaks again so that there are at least two full passes of thread.

13 Bring the ending tail of the thread out of the same space as the starting tail. Take out the thread slack and tie a knot with the two tails. Run the tails in opposite directions through the handle or netting and trim.

finish

14 To create the closure, sew the 12-mm pearl to the center front, about ½ inch (1.3 cm) down from the top edge (photo 2). Anchor the pearl in place with one 11° lustered transparent crystal bead. Using beading nylon, bring a double thread out of the center back hem, directly aligned with the pearl.

15 Add more 11° crystal beads until the resulting loop will fit neatly around the pearl without pulling it upward. Run the thread back into the hem and reverse direction; make as many thread passes as will fit through the beads, then secure the thread tail in the hem and trim it.

handle with netting

An elegant little bag with a button tab, this project looks more difficult to make than it really is. (You don't need to tell anyone else that.) Make the pattern offered here, or fill in the blank chart for this project on page 127 to chart your own direction.

a peach of a bag

a peach of a bag

before you begin

Here you'll learn to create a button tab using interior corners, which will be formed by crocheting three stitches together. The bottom portion will be crocheted, and then the tab portion will be added separately. The step-up position will be move from the center back in the lower portion to the side in the upper portion. Pay attention to those colored marks on the stitch chart; they indicate specific steps in the process of crocheting this small piece.

what you need

beads

All Czech 11° beads:

 #06013 opaque bone
(235 beads)

 #BL99 Ceylon peach
(3,758 beads)

 #17059 silver-lined gold AB
(422 beads)

 #63130 opaque lustered turquoise
(285 beads)

 #23220 silk medium lavender
(52 beads)

additional materials and tools

#12 perle cotton, peach, 5 g

Metal button with shank,
½ inch (1.3 cm) in diameter

Satin twist cord for handle,
24 inches (61 cm) (optional)

Crochet hooks, beading needles,
and scissors

Sewing thread and needle for sewing
on button (optional)

what you do

make the lower portion

1 Thread on at least the lower 14 rounds of the area indicated on the Lower Portion Chart. You'll be making increases in this section, and it will be easier if you don't need to attach a new thread. Don't add beads in the positions marked with red or green squares.

2 The starting chain is 59 stitches. Join with a slip stitch.

3 Make 14 single crochet with a bead, then two single crochet without beads. These two spaces are shown on the chart as red squares. Make 27 single crochet with beads, then two without. Finish the round with 14 single crochet with beads, then step up.

4 In the next round, make 14 single crochet with beads, then two single crochet with beads in each of the next two stitches; these will be the stitches without beads. By making your first increase in unbeaded single crochets, you will soften the increase corner so it has a more rounded appearance.

5 Make 27 single crochet with beads, then two single crochet with beads in each of the next two stitches; again, these are the unbeaded stitches. Complete the round with 14 single crochet with beads, then step up.

6 You'll notice that the work has now been shaped to create "corners." In the next eight rounds, you'll make four increases, with two right next to each other on both sides of the design, at the emerging corners. The step-up will always take place in the center back of the growing work.

7 In the round following the last increase, single crochet with a bead in all stitches and step up.

8 In the next round, single crochet with a bead in all stitches, but make one chain without a bead in the two positions marked with green squares.

9 You've now established the shape of the bag. Continue threading and crocheting until the entire charted area is crocheted, making one decrease at the orange squares. Cut and secure your thread within the crochet.

lower portion chart

continue the rows across the gaps in the chart

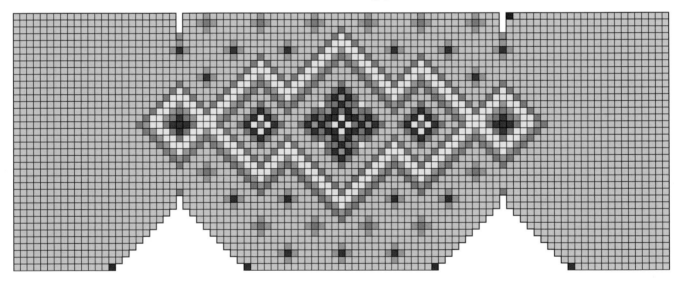

KEY

opaque bone (235)

Ceylon peach (3,758)

silver-lined gold AB (422)

opaque lustered turquoise (285)

silk medium lavender (52)

■ In crocheting, make one single crochet without a bead

■ Increase one by crocheting two stitches in the chain

■ Decrease by crocheting one stitch into two

a peach of a bag

make the upper portion

10 Thread about 800 peach beads (about 1½ teaspoons [7.4 ml]). Pull up a loop in the position marked by a blue square on the stitch chart. Chain one and make your first single crochet in the same space. Now work toward the center back (single crochet with beads) until you reach the previous step-up point (shown by a blue line in figure 1). Make six chains with beads (shown in green) and 20 chains without beads (shown in red).

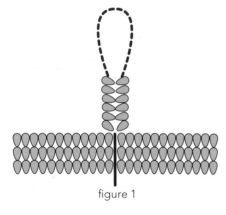

figure 1

11 Single crochet with a bead in each of the beaded chains you just added. Now work in single crochet with beads until you reach your new step-up point, shown by the blue square on the stitch chart. Join and step up.

12 Refer to figure 2, which shows the entire width of the back. Make 21 single crochet with beads. The next step is to create an interior corner. Pull up a loop in the next two single crochet and in the first of the beaded chains. Complete the single crochet using all the loops; the resulting stitch is shown in yellow on figure 2. Now make single crochets with beads in the next five beaded chains. Work 24 single crochet with beads in the 18-chain space. Make one single crochet with a bead in each of the next five beaded chains.

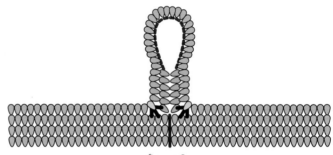

figure 2

13 Create an interior corner again, using loops from the last beaded chain and the next two beaded single crochet. Continue around to complete the round, then join and step up again.

14 Following figure 3, start the next round with 20 single crochet with beads, then repeat the interior corner. Make 13 single crochet with beads, then make one increase by crocheting two stitches in the next stitch (both with beads). Make four single crochet with beads, then increase in the next stitch. Make 13 single crochet with beads, then repeat the interior corner. Complete the round and step up.

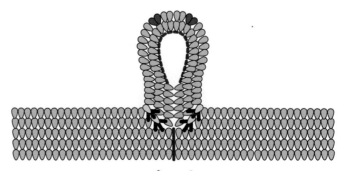

figure 3

15 In the next round, start with 19 single crochet with beads, then make the interior corner. Increase as indicated by the purple stitches in figure 4. Mirror the increase and the interior corner on the opposite side. Complete the round and step up.

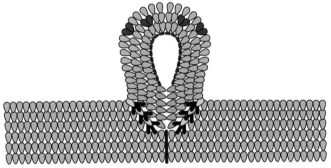

figure 4

16 In the next round, start with 18 single crochet with beads. Make the interior corner, then make just one single crochet with bead. Skip the next stitch (shown in pink in figure 5), then follow the illustration, increasing at the purple stitches. Mirror the increase, the skipped stitch, and the interior corner, then complete the round. Join with a slip stitch, but do not step up; cut your thread and secure it within the crochet.

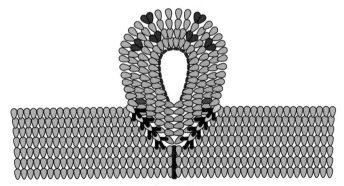

figure 5

17 Thread on 115 silver-lined gold AB beads. Attach the thread at the step-up and make 17 single crochet with beads. Make an interior corner, then crochet around the tab without increases. Mirror the interior corner, then single crochet with beads around the top edge. Join with a slip stitch, then cut the thread and secure it within the crochet.

18 Sew the bottom edges together with the perle cotton. Sew the button in place (either with perle cotton or regular sewing thread) so it is positioned properly to fit through the buttonhole with the tab sitting neatly on the front of the bag. If desired, add a satin-twist cord handle by stitching it inside the top corners of the bag.

It's beader's choice: You can make this useful little case with a different pattern on each side, or follow the additional charts and bead counts for wrapping either pattern all the way around.

aztec &
bargello case

aztec & bargello case

before you begin

This is another simple flat piece to make, where the basic instruction is "crochet and go!" The main beads list and first chart give you the beads you'll need to make the two sides in different patterns. I've also provided two charts with bead counts for making a case with all one pattern. You won't need to make a lining here because the crochet fabric is soft and supple.

what you need

beads

Bead counts for one side Aztec, one side Bargello:

 Czech #BL584 11°, silk eggshell (1,451 beads)

Czech #BL564 11°, silk salmon (1,555 beads)

Czech #01750 11°, silk copper (1,096 beads)

 Toho #55 11°, opaque turquoise (1,266 beads)

Czech #33060 11°, opaque cobalt (866 beads)

additional materials and tools

#12 perle cotton in a neutral color such as beige or tan, about 10 g

Crochet hooks, beading needles, and scissors

Sewing needle

what you do

1 Choose which of the three patterns (Aztec and Bargello, Aztec Only, or Bargello Only) you'd like to make, and gather the beads for that design. Load your beads in sections, with eight to 10 rows per threading.

2 You'll use the tail thread from your initial chain of 82 to sew the bottom edge together, so leave about 8 inches (20.3 cm) of perle cotton as you make your slip knot and starting chain.

3 Working from bottom to top, crochet the rows in the stitch chart.

4 Following the instructions in the Closing an Open End section (page 27), use the starting tail thread to sew the bottom seam of the case closed.

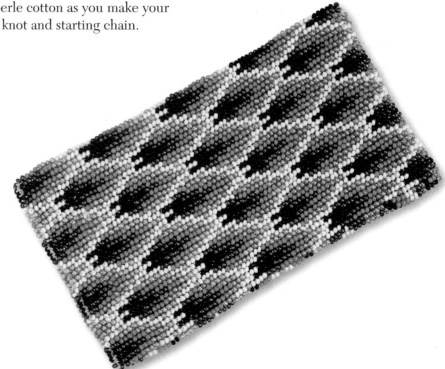

aztec & bargello case

aztec and bargello chart

KEY

silk eggshell (1,451)

silk salmon (1,555)

silk copper (1,096)

opaque turquoise (1,266)

opaque cobalt (866)

aztec only chart

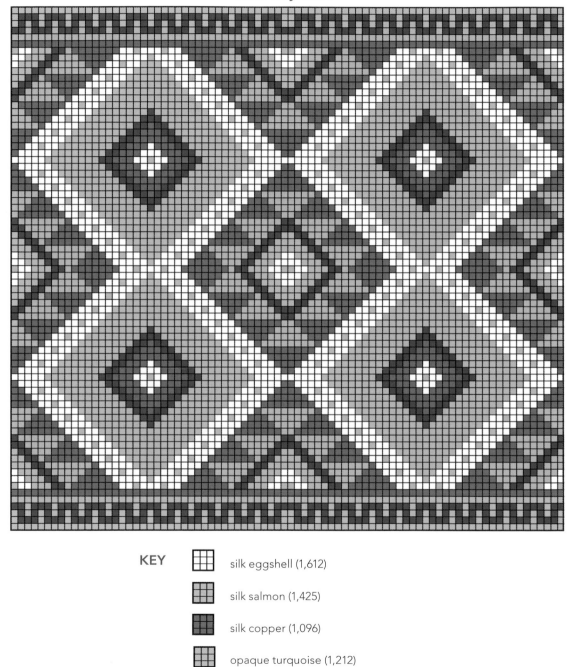

KEY

▦ silk eggshell (1,612)

▦ silk salmon (1,425)

▦ silk copper (1,096)

▦ opaque turquoise (1,212)

▦ opaque cobalt (958)

bargello only chart

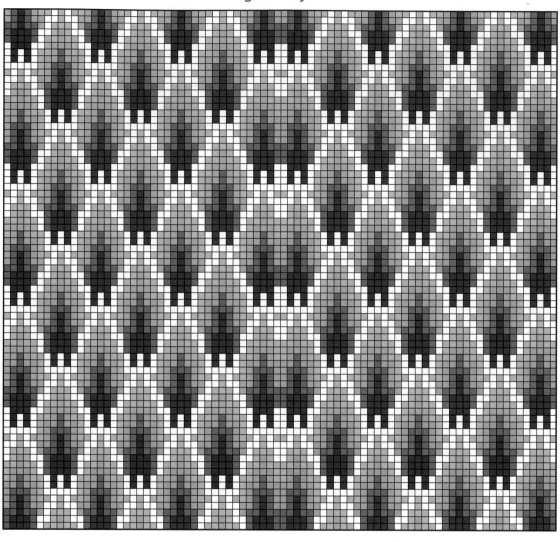

KEY

silk eggshell (1,290)

silk salmon (1,684)

silk copper (1,256)

opaque turquoise (1,320)

opaque cobalt (764)

 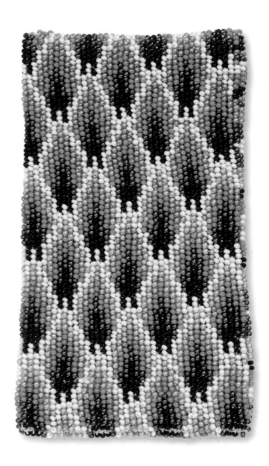

tip

Dress up the top edge of the case with an attractive button and loop closure.

what's in a name?

"Bargello" is a traditional canvas-stitching technique in which long threads are run on a straight vertical path in patterns that are densely geometric or flame-like—hence the alternate name "flame stitch." It's a technique often used for upholstering chair cushions or decorative pillows.

leather bargello bag

Only the top and handles of this sophisticated bag are crocheted; the golden leather and soft lining provide a perfect accompaniment.

before you begin

Because the total amount of crochet needed to make this bag is fairly small, you can thread each side all at once—no sections needed! The backs of the crocheted bands will be unbeaded crochet. In the finishing process, these unbeaded backs will be covered in lining fabric.

what you need

beads

For the crocheted bands:

 Toho #176F 11°, matte Capri blue AB (385 beads)

 Czech #59145 11°, dark metallic copper (355 beads)

 Czech #18549 11°, galvanized chrome with stable finish (315 beads)

 Czech #59142 11°, metallic brass (310 beads)

 Czech #18581 11°, galvanized bright gold charlotte with stable finish (290 beads)

24 faceted fire-polished beads, half-silvered, 4 mm

For the handles:

 Toho #176F 11°, matte Capri blue AB (310 beads)

 Czech #18581 11°, galvanized bright gold charlotte with stable finish (930 beads)

4 matte aqua Czech glass rondelles, 8 x 6 mm

additional materials and tools

For the crochet bands:

#12 crochet cotton, tan or light ochre, one 2.5-gram ball

4 x 7 inches (10.2 x 17.8 cm) of shirt weight cardboard

For the handles:

26 inches (66 cm) of 18-gauge brass wire

For the bag:

Gold soft leather (lambskin or kidskin), one piece 8½ x 12½ inches (21.6 x 31.8 cm)

Soft lightweight lining fabric such as silk or acetate, ¼ yard (22.9 cm)

Ordinary sewing thread in a matching color

Tools:

Crochet hooks, beading needles, and scissors

Sewing needle

Wire cutters

Round-nose pliers

Chain-nose pliers

what you do

crochet the bands

1 To make the front crocheted band, follow the topmost stitch chart on page 58. Thread on the side all at once, with no sectioning needed. The initial chain will be 120 stitches. Join with a slip stitch; chain one, (single crochet) without a bead in the same chain (step up).

2 Single crochet 30 more without beads (a total of 31 unbeaded single crochet).

3 Crochet 59 with single crochet beads; this should complete one row of the charted pattern.

leather bargello bag

4 Crochet 30 single crochet without beads. Step up again as before. You'll notice that the unbeaded side of the stitching has two more stitches than the beaded side, and that the step-up does not fall exactly in the center back.

5 Crochet all rounds in this manner, with 59 beaded single crochet on one side and a total of 61 unbeaded single crochet on the other. Leave a thread tail at least 12 inches (30.5 cm) long to use in finishing.

6 To make the back crocheted band, follow the bottom chart at right and repeat the same process you did in steps 1 through 5.

front band chart

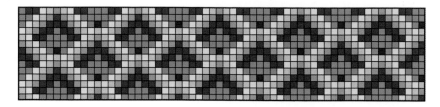

back band chart

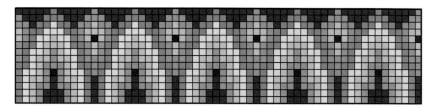

KEY

matte Capri blue AB (385)

dark metallic copper (355)

galvanized chrome with stable finish (315)

metallic brass (310)

galvanized bright gold charlotte with stable finish (290)

faceted fire-polished beads (24)

1

finish the bands

7 For each crocheted band, use the leftover thread tail to sew the top edges together (*not* the bottom edge) using small invisible stitches (photo 1). Take care not to pull too tightly or the top edge may pucker and shorten.

8 Cut two pieces of shirt-weight cardboard that are about ¼ inch (6 mm) longer than the crocheted bands and about ⅛ inch (3 mm) narrower.

9 Open the bottom edge of the bands and insert the cardboard pieces (photo 2); stretch the crochet outward to accommodate the length of the cardboard. If any cardboard protrudes from the open bottom, check that the piece is all the way inside. If there is still any excess, pull the cardboard out and trim until it fits properly (as it does in photo 3), taking care not to cut the crochet.

make the leather bag

10 Fold the leather piece in half, right side inward. Sew side seams about two-thirds of the way up, curving at the base as shown in the illustration below.

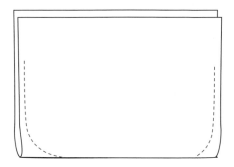

11 Trim ½ inch (1.3 cm) off the top of the lining fabric so it will fit inside the leather piece, then sew it in the same manner as the leather.

12 Trim and notch the curved corners as shown in photos 4 and 5.

2

3

4

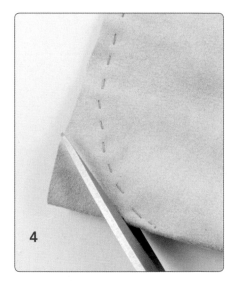

5

leather bargello bag

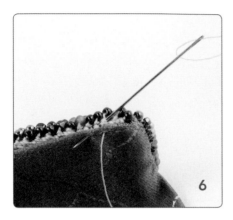

6

add the lining

13 Cut the lining fabric about ½ inch (1.3 cm) larger all around than the size of the back of the crocheted bands. Press the top and side edges under and slip-stitch to the back of the lining so the bottom edge is still open (photo 6).

14 If your lining fabric is pretty on both sides, have some fun and use both sides, as in this piece. Run a thread ½ inch (1.3 cm) from each of the open edges of the lining fabric, then gather so it's the same size as the open edge of the crocheted band (photo 7).

7

15 Tuck the lining into the open band, between the lining and the un-beaded crochet, then stitch the bottom edge of the band lining over the top edge of the bag lining (photo 8).

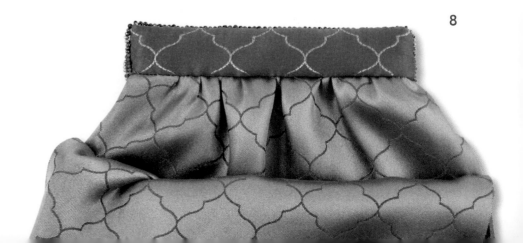

8

9

assemble the bag

16 Gather the leather in the same manner as the lining; slip the lining inside the leather. Slip the gathered leather inside the front of the crocheted band, between the cardboard and the crochet (photo 9). The leather may tend to slip out; hold it in place with clothespins if necessary. Tack the front edge of the crochet to the leather roughly at the gather line.

17 When you're satisfied that the leather is secure within the bands, stitch the open edges of the lining and the leather together at the side openings (photo 10).

10

tip

You can add a magnetic or snap closure in the center inside of the crocheted bands, but the weight of the bag will likely keep the bag closed as you carry it.

leather bargello bag

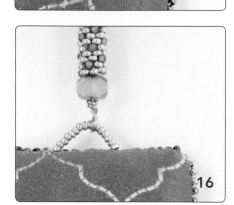

11

make the handle

18 Following the directions for tubular crochet found on page 24, crochet two identical tubes following the pattern shown in photo 11 until you have completed 110 rounds for each tube (photo 12). Secure the threads within the weave of the tube, avoiding the center channel, which will later be filled with wire.

12

19 Cut two pieces of wire, about 3 inches (7.6 cm) longer overall than the tubes. Slip one piece of wire through each tube; it's helpful to twist the tube as you push the wire through. Add one rondelle to each end of the tubes (photo 13).

20 Using the round-nose and chain-nose pliers, make wrapped loops outside the rondelles (photo 14). Make sure that the handles are as close in size as possible.

14

13

15

16

21 Bring a doubled thread out of the top edge, about ½ inch (1.3 cm) from the outer corner. The knot shown in photo 15 will hold the initial thread in place, but it will be trimmed off (carefully!) later. Pick up 15 bright gold 11° charlotte beads; run through one of the wire loops. Skip about ½ inch (1.3 cm) on the top edge and run the thread into the crochet. Reverse direction and make two more passes of thread through all the beads. Repeat on both sides until the handles are complete.

With this case, you can hold even
the largest wraparound sunglasses.
Or just slip your checkbook into the pouch,
and you'll never have to hunt for it again.

spectacle case

spectacle case

before you begin

As with other flat projects, the front and back of this bag are crocheted together at the same time, arranged as shown here. The two charts are the same number of units high and wide (99 x 47). The two sides use some—but not all—of the same beads, so each has its own color symbol chart.

what you need

beads

For the paisley side:

Czech 11° #06013, opaque bone (2,968 beads)

Czech 11° #26210, opaque pale orchid (1,360 beads)

Czech 11° #63000, light aqua (202 beads)

Miyuki 11° #2025, opaque medium amethyst (350 beads)

Czech 11° #23020, opaque dark amethyst (1,104 beads)

Czech 11° #17020, silver-lined gold (2.030 beads)

Toho 11° #127, opaque dusty rose (798 beads)

Czech 11° #37154, light Ceylon green (64 beads)

Czech 11° #BL579, silk medium turquoise (430 beads)

Czech 11° #53240, opaque medium green (418 beads)

Toho 11° #127, opaque dusty rose (1,824 beads)

Czech 11° #BL579, silk medium turquoise (40 beads)

Czech 11° #23020, opaque dark amethyst (1,134 beads)

Czech 11° #37154, light Ceylon green (564 beads)

Czech 11° #63080, opaque denim blue (620 beads)

additional materials and tools

#12 perle cotton in a neutral color such as tan or beige

Crochet hooks, beading needles, and scissors

For the senna side:

Czech 11° #23980, opaque black (3,298 beads)

Czech 11° #26210, opaque pale orchid (1,000 beads)

Czech 11° #17020, silver-lined gold (408 beads)

what you do

1 The initial chain for this project is 94 stitches. You'll be stitching this project in the round, but you'll flatten the rounded piece at the step-up, which will fall naturally at the side, emulating a seam, and forcing a seam on the opposite side.

2 Thread in 10-row (or fewer) sections and crochet as charted.

3 When the crochet is complete, add a four-round hem at the top edge. When the hem rounds are complete, cut the crochet thread tail at least 12 inches (30.5 cm) long. Pull this cut thread through the last loop to secure it, then use the tail to stitch the bottom edges together.

tip

Here's a fun variation of this design: Work the pattern with the seams on the short sides and add a zipper to the top, and you've made a case for carrying cosmetic items in your purse. See the Phoenix Carryall project on page 34 for instructions on adding a zipper.

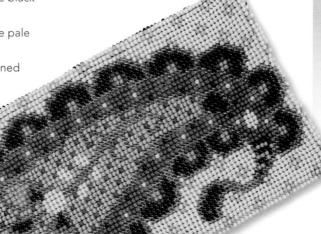

paisley side chart   senna side chart

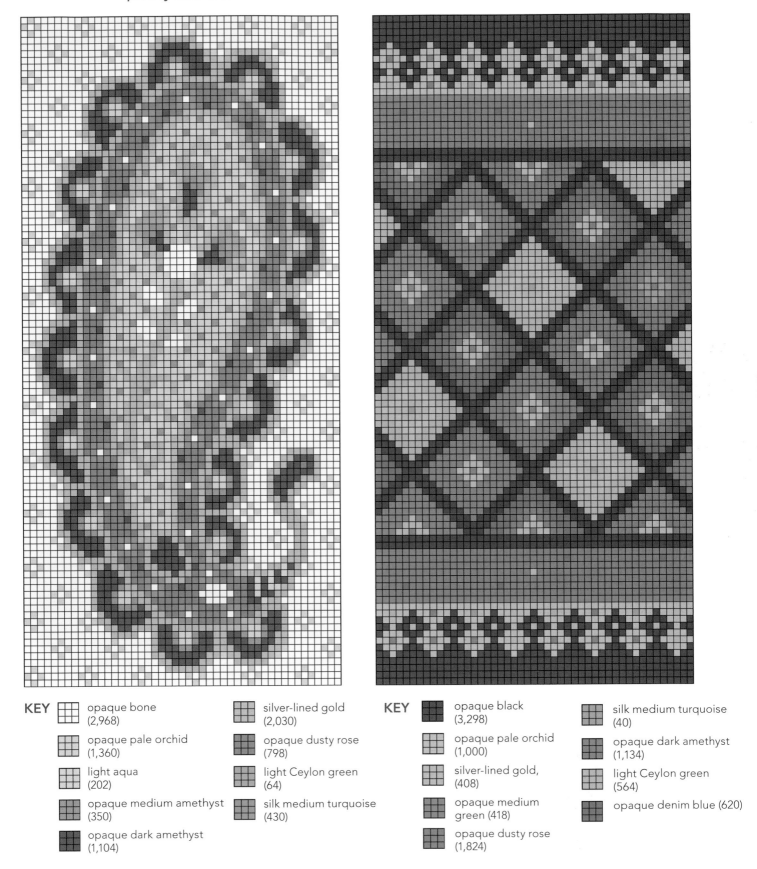

KEY ▦ opaque bone
(2,968)

▦ opaque pale orchid
(1,360)

▦ light aqua
(202)

▦ opaque medium amethyst
(350)

▦ opaque dark amethyst
(1,104)

▦ silver-lined gold
(2,030)

▦ opaque dusty rose
(798)

▦ light Ceylon green
(64)

▦ silk medium turquoise
(430)

KEY ▦ opaque black
(3,298)

▦ opaque pale orchid
(1,000)

▦ silver-lined gold,
(408)

▦ opaque medium
green (418)

▦ opaque dusty rose
(1,824)

▦ silk medium turquoise
(40)

▦ opaque dark amethyst
(1,134)

▦ light Ceylon green
(564)

▦ opaque denim blue (620)

Chapter 5

hex-based patterns

Round and round you go, and the results are these elegant beauties,

using the simple hex-based technique.

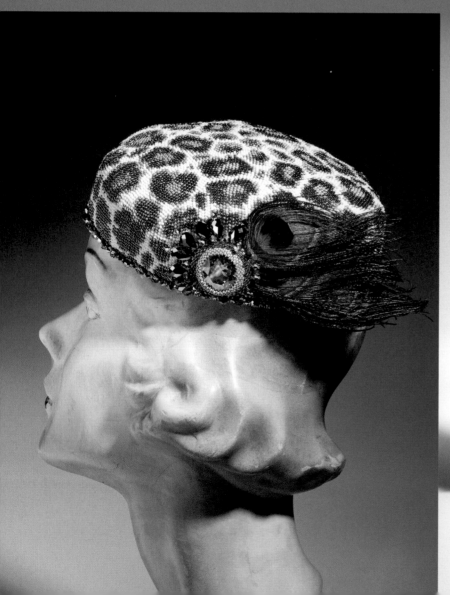

treasure box
pineapple drawstring bag
paisley pouch
chatelaine
leopard-skin pillbox hat
lotus purse

This simple but beautiful pattern makes for a special gift.
You can enclose another item inside for even more treasure.

treasure
box

treasure box

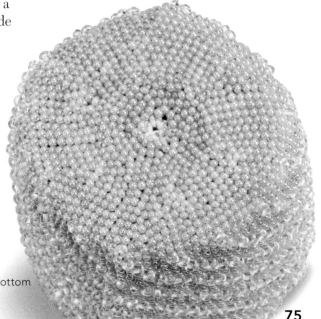

before you begin

This project is shown in a monochromatic version. If you'd like to try making it with a combination of two or more colors, make a copy of the blank template on page 126 and fill it in with whatever design you'd like.

what you need

beads

11° seed beads, one color
(5,344 beads, or about 11 g)

8° seed beads, one contrasting
or complementary color
(544 beads, or about 1.1 g)

additional materials and tools

#12 perle cotton in a coordinating color

Nonwoven stabilizer

Lightweight lining fabric in a coordinating color

Sewing needle and ordinary sewing thread in a matching color

Small amount of polyester batting

Crochet hooks, beading needles, and long-handled scissors

what you do

crochet the base

1 Thread on 810 11° beads. Crochet a beaded hex base (page 28) that is 16 rounds out (96 stitches in the perimeter). Join at the end with a slip stitch; secure the thread within the crochet.

2 Following the stitch chart on page 71, thread on the 11° and 8° beads for the sides. This project is 35 rounds high; you can thread on five sections of seven rounds each. Pull up a loop anywhere in the outside round of the hex base.

3 Crochet the 35 beaded rounds without any increase. Add a six-round unbeaded hem.

crochet the box top

4 Thread on 1,734 11° beads.

5 Crochet a beaded hex base that is 17 rounds out (102 stitches in the perimeter). At this point, stop increasing; add eight rounds of single crochet with beads. Now add six rounds of unbeaded crochet.

view from the bottom

treasure box

finish the box base

6 Cut two pieces of stabilizer that are roughly the same height as the box side, and roughly the same length as the circumference of the box base (photo 1).

7 Trim the two pieces so they fit together as shown in figure 1. The outside layer will be slightly larger than the inside layer. Baste the two pieces together with the sewing needle and ordinary sewing thread and force them inside the box.

figure 1

8 Stretch the crocheted box upward until the stabilizer is completely inside the crochet. Roll the hem over the edge of the stabilizer and turn it down inside the box. Baste the hem in place through all layers with the sewing needle and thread, making sure that the stitches are not visible on the outside (photo 2).

9 Bunch the lining fabric and push it down into the box until it touches the bottom of the box. Using long-bladed scissors, cut the bunched fabric about ½ inch (1.3 cm) above the top of the box (photo 3). The resulting cut edge will be rough.

10 Trim the roughly cut edge. It doesn't need to be perfect, just relatively smooth (photo 4).

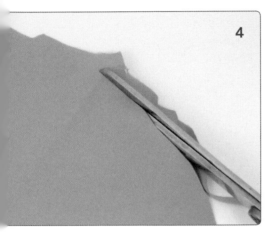

4

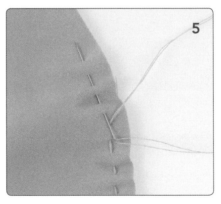

11 Run a gathering thread all around the perimeter of the lining, about ⅜ inch (9.5 mm) inside the edge (photo 5).

5

12 Gather the edge of the lining. Place the gathered lining inside the box. Fold the cut edge at the gather line so the edge disappears between the box and the lining. Sew the lining to the base along the top edge, using small invisible stitches.

stitch chart

finish the top

13 Cut a piece of stabilizer about the same diameter as the finished top (photo 6). Use the stabilizer as a template to cut a piece of lining fabric.

6

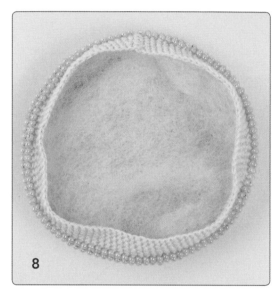

8

14 Baste the lining to the stabilizer around the outside edge (photo 7, below left).

15 Place the batting inside the crocheted top (photo 8).

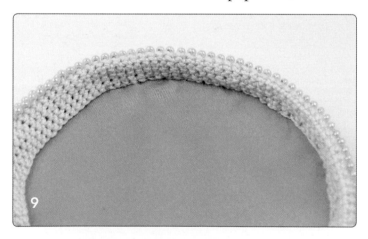

7

9

16 Place the stabilizer and lining over the batting so the lining faces out. Fold the hem of the top inside and push it out so an edge is formed. Baste the edge all around with invisible stitches (photo 9).

The pineapple motif encircling the sides of this project gives it a folk-art feel; the drawstring around the top makes it a handy carryall for all sorts of small items.

pineapple drawstring bag

pineapple drawstring bag

before you begin

You can use any two complementary colors you'd like here. Make sure there is enough contrast between the two colors so the pattern will emerge. One possibility: a matte-finish bead as the background color and a shiny-surfaced bead for the image color. Traditional pineapple colors of light yellow (background) and darker green (image) would be wonderful too. Or you can use the blank version of this chart on page 126 and create a design with as many colors as you like.

what you need

beads

 Czech 11° #69010, copper-lined aqua (3,342 beads, or 34 g [one hank])

 Czech 11° #78109, silver-lined crystal AB (3,120 beads, or 31 g [slightly less than one hank])

additional materials and tools

#12 perle cotton, light gray, 20 g

1/8-inch (3 mm) satin rat-tail cord for drawstring, 30 inches (76.2) long

Lightweight lining fabric (optional)

Crochet hooks, beading needles, and scissors

what you do

crochet the bag

1 Thread on 10 grams (about 2 teaspoons) of the 11° aqua beads. Create a hex base (see page 28) that has a perimeter of 120 beads.

2 Following the stitch chart, thread in sections of six to eight rounds. Pull up a loop in any bead of the perimeter of the hex base and crochet in rounds, working upward until you reach the fourth round from the top of the chart.

tip

You can find crochet abbreviations on page 127, but here's a little reminder about the ones used in step 3: scb = single crochet bead; ch = chain.

create the buttonholes

3 The blank spaces on the chart (the fourth row from the top) represent the buttonhole eyelets for the drawstring. In that row, thread on only 60 beads before placing the marker. Crochet as follows: After stepping up, make 3 scb, then *ch 3, skip 3 scb and scb in the next 3 scb.* Repeat between *s all around; end with ch 3. Join the ending chain with a slip stitch to the first scb. In the next round, ch 1, scb in the first scb, then scb in all scb, and make 3 scb in all ch 3 spaces all around. Join with slip stitch to the first scb of the round. Work the remaining rounds normally; end by joining with a slip stitch in the first scb of the round. Cut your thread; secure the thread end by pulling the thread all the way through. Bury the thread end within the crochet.

finish

4 When the crochet is complete, add the drawstring. First cut the satin cord into two equal sections. Tape one end of each piece, so it looks like the tip of a shoelace (photo 1). Run the taped end through half the openings with one piece (photo 2), and half with the other piece. Tie the adjacent ends together with a simple knot; tighten the knot before trimming the ends. Secure all your thread ends within the inside crochet and trim, taking care not to cut the crochet.

5 If you wish to line the bag, use a lightweight fabric and attach it with small stitches below the drawstring row.

bag chart

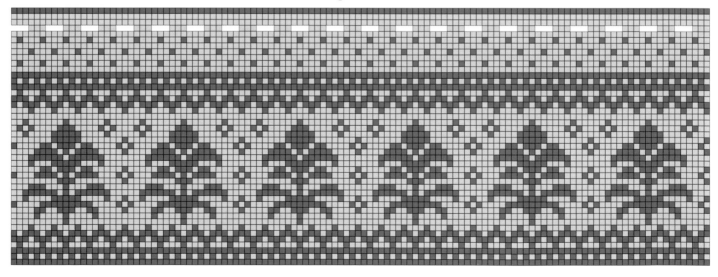

paisley pouch

Let it rain: Shiny raindrop beads add a defining border around the top and bottom of this chic little bag.

paisley pouch

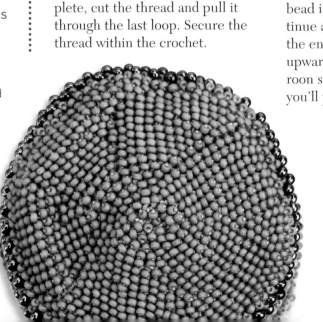

before you begin

This pouch bag is closed at the top with a drawstring through buttonholes. The buttonholes are placed precisely so the top of the bag will "fold" inward, creating recessed sides with lots of room to carry your evening things.

what you need

Beads

 Miyuki #2032 11°, matte medium olive (3,488 beads [35 g])

 Czech #23560 11°, silk light olive (1,079 beads [11 g])

 Miyuki #2015 11°, matte black olive (883 beads [9 g])

 Czech #BL584 11°, silk pale olive (816 beads [9 g])

 Toho #996 11°, gold-lined light peridot AB (280 beads [3 g])

 Czech #59155 8° raindrop beads, green iris (192 beads)

additional materials and tools

#12 perle cotton, light sage, 10 g

¼-inch (6 mm) satin twist cord, sage green, 24 inches (61 cm) long

Crochet hooks, beading needles, and scissors

Non-water-based glue (optional)

what you do

1 Create a hex base (see page 28) using the Miyuki olive beads; see how the finished base looks at right. Work until there are 96 beads in the perimeter of the hex base.

2 When the hex base is complete, cut the thread and pull it through the last loop. Secure the thread within the crochet.

3 Thread on the pattern shown on the stitch chart on page 79 in sections of seven to 10 rounds. Pull up a loop anywhere in the perimeter of the hex base, chain one, and single crochet with a bead in the same space. Continue all around, stepping up at the end of the round, then work upward until you reach the maroon squares on the chart, where you'll place the buttonholes.

create the buttonholes

4 Near the top of the bag, around the last section you crochet, you'll create the open holes to pass the braided drawstring through. Each maroon square represents one chain stitch worked without a bead. Start that round with six scb, then chain 3 without beads. Skip three scb and scb in the next eight scb. Ch 3 without beads again; skip three scb, then scb in the next eight scb. Continue in this manner following the chart; note that the center group has 12 scb instead of eight. This group will land at the center front of the finished pouch. In the next round, scb in all scb, and work 3 scb in each ch 3 space all around, for a total of 96 stitches. Thereafter, work as previously, making one scb in each scb.

finish

5 When the crochet is complete, secure all threads within the interior fibers of the pouch and trim. You don't need to line this pouch, but if you do, you must position the lining below the buttonholes and secure it with small stitches.

6 To add the drawstring, put tape on the ends of the twisted braid (or leave the tape on if it's already there). Insert one end of the taped braid through one of the holes on either side of the back joint; insert the other end through the other hole near the back joint (photo 1). Weave each end through four holes so the two ends emerge from the center front on either side of the 12-scb group from step 4.

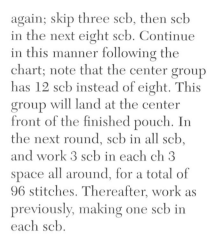

7 Tie the two taped ends together with a tight knot so the knot lands about 2 inches (5.1 cm) from the taped ends (photo 2). If desired, place a dot of glue on the inside of the knot before tightening, using a non-water-based glue with a fine-tipped applicator. When the knot is tight, trim off the tape and loosen the fibers of the braid. Press the braid with a steam iron; trim again if needed. You may need to clean up the edge of the fiber from time to time over the life of the pouch.

Bottom

Top

	silk pale olive (816)		medium matte olive (3,488)
	silk light olive (1,079)		matte black olive (883)
	gold-lined light peridot AB (280)		green iris raindrops (192)

Traditional chatelaines, used by the lady of the household
to carry her keys, were often pinned to a dress bodice or waist.
This version has a strap you can attach to a belt loop
on your jeans or the strap of your handbag.

chatelaine

chatelaine

before you begin

As pictured here, this design uses very few colors, but it's ripe for color experimentation. If you have a favorite patterned hex chart, use that to create the back and front of the bag. Quick and easy to create, this project makes an excellent gift.

what you need

beads

 Toho #1700 11°, 24k-gold-marbled opaque pale amethyst (primary color) (2,770 beads)

 Toho #325 11°, lustered dark amethyst gold (contrasting color) (403 beads)

 Czech #18581 13° charlotte, galvanized gold with stable finish (120 beads)

 Toho #221 8°, metallic bronze (86 beads)

additional materials and tools

#12 perle cotton, taupe

Beading nylon, 36 inches (91 cm)

12-mm disk pearl, center drilled

Crochet hooks, beading needles, and long-handled scissors

what you do

1 Crochet two hex bases (see page 28) as follows: Using 11° #1700s, work outward until you have 20 rounds, a total of 120 beaded single crochet around (photo 1). Leave a long tail of about 18 inches (45.7 cm) on one of the hexes; secure the tail within the crochet and trim it on the other.

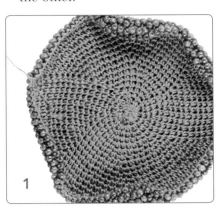

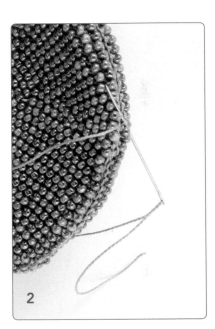

2 Press the hexes so they are flat; use your fingertips to round out the corners if necessary. Place the two pieces together, with the crochet side in and the beaded side out. Match up the increases on one to the increases on the other. Using the long tail, sew the two hexes together along four of the six edges (photo 2). Don't join them along the last two edges (photo 3).

chatelaine

3 Secure a 36-inch (91 cm) length of beading nylon at one end of the seam. Put five contrasting 11° beads on the thread; run the thread through the edge seam about two stitches' width away (photo 4). Run the thread back through the last 11° bead added, and tighten (photo 5).

4 Pick up four of the same 11° beads and run the thread through the seam, again about two stitches away (photo 6). Run back through the last 11° bead added (photo 7).

4

5

6

7

5 Continue in this manner, adding four 11° beads each time, working across one side of the unseamed opening until you almost reach the starting point. For the last group, pick up only three 11° beads of the same color, and run through the very first contrasting 11° bead added in the edging (photo 8). The other unseamed edge will remain undecorated.

6 Run through the seam below that 11° bead, then back through the first three 11° beads, exiting in the center 11° bead of the first group of five added (photo 9).

7 Pick up one contrasting 11° bead, one 8° bead, and one 13° charlotte bead (photo 10). Skip the charlotte and run back through the 8° bead. Pick up another contrasting 11° bead and run through the center bead of the next loop (photo 11). Repeat these peaks all around until you reach the starting point. Secure the thread and trim it.

8

9

10

11

chatelaine

make the closure

8 To create the strip for part of the closure, you'll use odd-count peyote stitch, a basic bead-weaving technique that yields a sturdy but flexible strip of beads. Even-count peyote can't be centered because it's asymmetrical. Follow the thread path shown in the diagram on page 85 to make the "figure eight" turn at the end of every other row. Secure a thread in the fiber of the undecorated edge three beads to one side of the increase point (photo 12).

12

9 Bring the thread out in the nearest stitch. You'll be creating a band of peyote stitch seven beads wide, centered over the increase point. Treat the seven edge beads as if they were the first row of peyote; add three beads over four beads (photo 13). Reverse direction and add another row. Continue weaving in peyote stitch until the band is 2¼ inches (5.7 cm) long, ending with a four-bead row (photo 14).

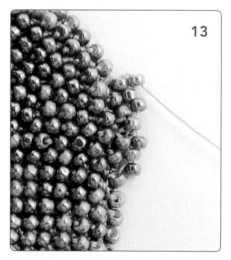

13

14

10 To create the loop that fits over the "button," pick up 23 11° beads of the primary color. Run through the bead at the opposite end of the row (photo 15). Working in peyote stitch, add one inner round of 13° charlottes. Weave through the band to bring the thread out of the second edge bead on either side. Add one round of the primary 11° beads around the outer edge (photo 16).

11 Weave through the band to bring the thread out of the third edge bead on either side. Add one outer round of 8° beads, then weave through until the thread emerges from the outer center of the toggle loop (photo 17). Add three contrasting 11° beads and four 8° beads. Skip the last three 8° beads and run through the first 8° bead added. Now add three more contrasting 11° beads, then run through the next outer edge 8° bead. Tighten the thread, then weave through to either edge of the band. Bring the thread out of the same edge bead as for the 8° bead (photo 18).

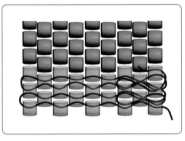

thread path

chatelaine

finish

12 Following the thread path marked on photo 19, add peaked edging to the sides of the band. Make sure that the peaks land directly opposite each other on the two sides for a neat appearance. Pick up one contrasting 11° bead, one 8° bead, and one 13° charlotte; skip the charlotte and run through the 8° bead. Pick up another contrasting 11° bead; skip one edge bead and run inward through the next. Pick up one charlotte and loop it to the edge as shown in the photo. Repeat on both sides until the edging reaches the undecorated open edge.

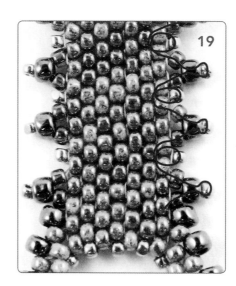

19

13 Sew the pearl button in place as shown in photo 20. Bring the thread out about ⅝ inch (1.6 cm) above the very center of the front hex. Add one 8° bead, the pearl button, and one contrasting 11° bead. Skip the 11° bead and run back through the pearl and the 8° bead into the hex front. Reverse direction and make at least two more passes of thread to secure the button. Secure the thread within the crochet and trim.

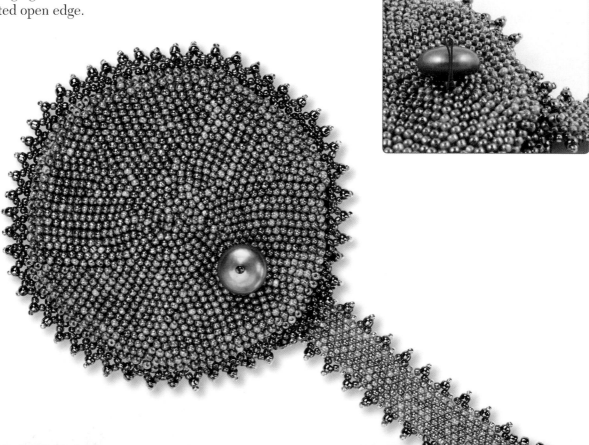

20

leopard-skin pillbox hat

This complex—and truly stunning—piece is not recommended for beginners to tapestry bead crochet. If you feel like you're ready to make it, though, you'll find it an irresistible challenge.

leopard-skin pillbox hat

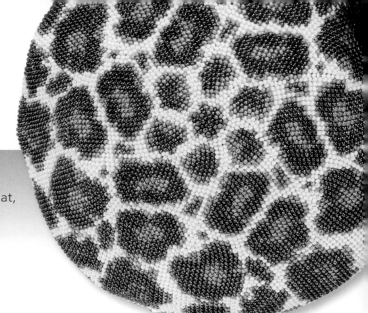

before you begin

This hat is really a large hex base pattern that forms a "crown" as the top of the hat. The crochet is then extended without increases to form the side of the hat, with the height of the wall 1½ inches (3.8 cm).

what you need

beads

 Toho #557F 11°, matte galvanized gold with stable finish (2,784 beads, plus additional if making the optional tubular band)

 Czech #59142 11°, metallic dark bronze (4,338 beads)

 Czech #06013 11°, opaque cream (3,510 beads)

 Czech #01770 11°, silk copper (2,304 beads, plus additional if making the optional tubular band)

additional materials and tools

#12 perle cotton, cream color, about 30 g

Nonwoven stabilizer, ½ yard (45.7 cm)

Lightweight polyester sheet batting, one 8-inch (20.3 cm) and one 12-inch (30.5 cm) circle

Acetate or polyester lining fabric in a coordinating color, ⅓ yard (30.5 cm)

Masking tape

Optional decorations: peacock feather, crystal cabochon, beads, headpins

Crochet hooks, beading needles, and scissors

what you do

1 Repeat each row shown in the stitch chart on the opposite page six times to complete one round. This chart represents one-sixth of the entire crocheted hat. Though the blue-outlined part appears triangular, it will work up into a rounded shape if repeated six times.

2 Work the hex following the chart; the center section is outlined in blue. Work all 31 rows of the center, then cut your thread and secure it within the crochet. Shift the step-up position by starting your next crochet section in the center of one repetition in the last round, rather than continuing to place the step-up in the same position. This maintains the rounded, rather than hexagonal, shape as much as possible.

3 Begin threading the part outlined in red. First, pull up a loop in the last round of the blue-outlined section in the stitch marked with a green square; this will be a cream bead. The adjoining green square of the red-outlined section is the first stitch of that section. This position is roughly in the center of one of the six repeats of the last round; it doesn't matter which repeat you use.

tip

To thread this design, I used a large white paper marker at the end of each round and a smaller colored paper marker at the end of each repeat. I placed a total of six markers for each round. I ended up with a lot of little pieces of paper on the floor, but it made the threading infinitely easier. You don't need to do this until about the seventh or eighth round, when it will become more difficult to keep track of your place. You should also keep the chart nearby to be sure you're crocheting correctly.

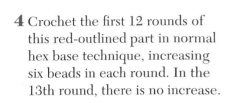

4 Crochet the first 12 rounds of this red-outlined part in normal hex base technique, increasing six beads in each round. In the 13th round, there is no increase.

5 In the 14th round, increase one bead in each hex section. As mentioned in the Tip box, markers after each repetition within the round are very helpful.

6 In the 15th round, do not increase. In the 16th round, increase one in each repeat.

7 From here on, all rounds will be crocheted without increases. When all the beads have been crocheted, work six unbeaded rounds to form a hem.

Green squares:
Use cream beads here

opaque cream (3510)

matte galvanized gold (stable finish) (2784)
(additional 500 needed to create the option tubular band)

silk copper (2304)
(additional 500 needed to create the optional tubular band)

metallic dark bronze (4338)

Center top of hat: Start crocheting here

leopard skin pillbox hat

2

create the hat form

8 You'll use nonwoven stabilizer to create a foundation with an inner and an outer layer for the hat. The three-point templates on page 93 each show one-quarter of a complete form. Make four copies of each template. Cut out and tape together the four copies of each to create an inner and an outer template, each with twelve spikes (as shown on page 92). The outer template will be slightly larger than the inner template.

9 Using the templates, cut out two sections of stabilizer, one for the outer form and one for the inner form.

10 Tape the side edges together (photo 1). An important note: The photos here show green tape for clarity, but you should use a neutral color tape, such as a light-colored masking tape.

11 Tape the points of the spikes together in the center (photo 2).

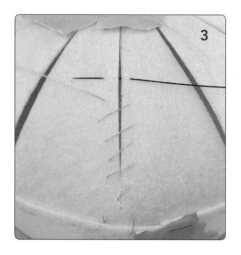

3

12 When both forms are taped, whip-stitch the spikes together along their side seams (photo 3).

13 Place the outer form over the inner form, in such a way that the whipped seams are not aligned. Use a few basting stitches to secure the two together.

14 Cut a strip of stabilizer 1¼ inches (3.2 cm) wide that is the length of the perimeter of the joined form plus ½ inch (1.3 cm). Wrap the strip around the edge of the form, tape the ends with a slight overlap (photo 4), and baste the strip around the outer edge of the form to stabilize the side walls.

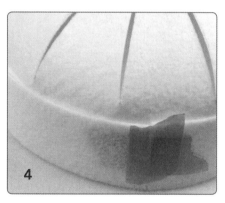

4

15 Stretch the thin polyester batting over the entire form, then stretch the crocheted hat over the form. Tuck in the polyester batting so that it doesn't protrude. Using large stitches, baste the lower edge of the crochet so that two to three rows of crochet and the hem protrude below the form (photo 5). Wrap the hem inward and secure it to the form with back-and-forth invisible stitches.

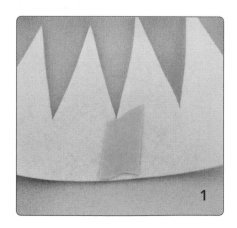

1

5

make the lining

16 Using the hat as a template, cut the lining fabric 2 inches (5.1 cm) larger all around than the perimeter of the hat.

17 Run a gathering stitch all around the outside edge, ½ inch (1.3 cm) in from the cut edge. To do this, sew ¼-inch (6 mm) stitches with a single or double thread all around. Notch the excess (photo 6), then pull on the thread to "ruffle" the fabric until the gathered edge is roughly the same size as the inner edge of the hat. Secure the gather with a few overstitches of the gathering thread, then trim it.

6

18 If the hat is floppy, you can use a section of plastic soft drink bottle to stiffen it (photo 7). Cut a piece that spans the inside top of the hat and baste it in place before adding the batting.

7

19 Place a thin layer of batting on the inside top of the hat, ending about 1 inch (2.5 cm) from the bottom edge. Shape the batting with your fingertips to press it into the hat.

20 Place the lining inside the hat. Turn the cut edge inside and stitch it in place along the edge of the hat with invisible hem stitches.

add the decorative band

21 To create a decorative band for the lower edge, stitch a six-around tube of bead crochet (see page 24). Thread on beads in this pattern: one Toho #557F matte galvanized gold, two Czech #01770 silk copper.

22 Repeat until you have about 3 yards (2.7 m) of threaded beads. Crochet the tube in six-around until it fits comfortably around the base of the hat; you may have threaded too many beads, or you may need to add more, depending on your stitch tension. Join the ends of the tube invisibly (see page 25) and stitch the circular band all around the lower edge of the hat using invisible stitches.

add decorations

23 The pictured hat has a decorative trim of crystals and seed beads around the top edge of the tubular band, and a crystal brooch with three peacock feathers attached. Other suggestions include marabou trim around the lower edge instead of tubular bead crochet, or a geisha-type stickpin. Have fun finishing the hat and wearing it!

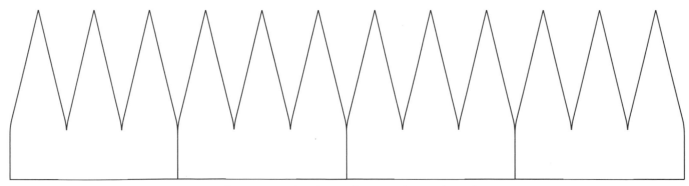

tape four copies of each template together as shown here

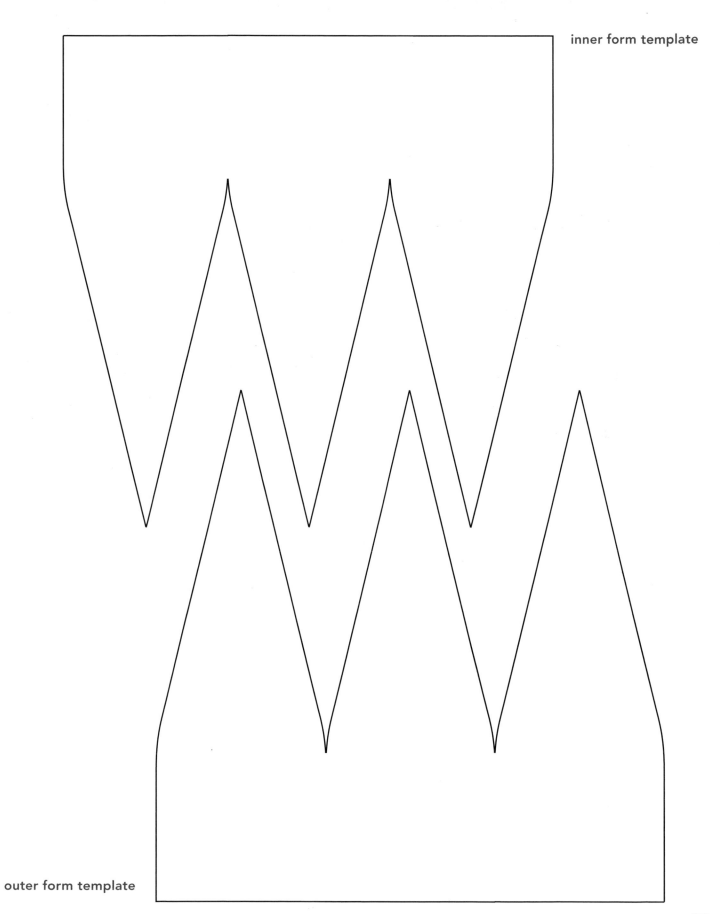

inner form template

outer form template

lotus
purse

This wonderful bag designed and crocheted by Lauren Miller uses the same evocative lotus blossom three times around.

lotus purse

before you begin

The base for this bag is a simple hex. After completing the hex base, you'll thread on three repetitions of each round. You should do five or six rows per section. Eyelets are used to create the openings for the satin drawstring.

what you need

beads

 Czech #67150 11°, silver-lined deep aqua (3,039 beads)

 Czech #78109 11°, silver-lined crystal AB (2,841 beads)

Czech #BL691 11°, lustered deep green (906 beads)

 Czech #BL586 11°, silk lichen green (816 beads)

 Czech #68105 11°, copper-lined crystal (810 beads)

Toho #23 11°, silver-lined light aqua (384 beads)

Czech #89010 11°, silver-lined tangerine (192 beads)

Czech #29010 11°, copper-lined amethyst (2,190 beads)

additional materials and tools

#12 perle cotton, gray

1/8-inch (3 mm) gold satin rat-tail cord for drawstring, 20 inches (50.8) long

Crochet hooks, beading needles, and scissors

what you do

1 Follow the general directions for creating a hex base (page 28). To begin, use the copper-lined amethyst beads and work until there are 144 stitches around (24 in each hex section).

2 Change to lichen green beads for one round, still increasing so there are 150 stitches. Increase again in the next round (156 stitches) using the lustered deep green beads. Add one final increase round (162 stitches) of copper-lined amethyst beads. This completes the hex base as seen at right.

tip

In placing your paper markers for this design, use a marker of one color to mark the end of one repeat and then a marker of another color to mark the end of the three-repeat round.

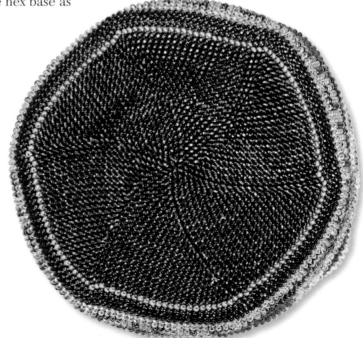

lotus purse

make the sides

3 The pattern in the stitch chart on the facing page is repeated three times around, with the bottom round stitched to the outer round of the hex base. You'll thread each row three times. Load only five rows at a time, because each row is quite long.

4 Pick up the threaded bottom section; pull up a loop anywhere in the last round of the hex base, chain one, sc with a bead in the same space as the pulled-up loop. Crochet the section without increases. Continue adding sections until you reach the eyelet round.

5 Add 18 eyelets in the top section. (Note that the chart has six eyelets and is repeated three times.) In the eyelet spaces, you don't thread on; the number of beads in the threaded round will be smaller. To form the eyelet, you need three rounds:

- In the first round, make five single crochet stitches without beads in the indicated positions. (These positions are marked in red on the chart and indicated in the bead symbol guide as well.)

- In the second round, chain five across each five-stitch space. Single crochet with a bead in the next four single crochet; these will have beads.

- In the third round, work five beaded single crochet into each chain-five space.

At this point, you'll have two rounds left to crochet with beads.

finish

6 When all the beads are crocheted, work four unbeaded rounds of single crochet to create the hem. Fold the hem over and secure it with invisible stitches, using the same thread as for the crochet itself.

7 Run the gold satin cord through the eyelets, weaving in and out. Start on one side of the step-up; end on the other side of the step-up. Tie a simple knot in the cord and trim the ends if needed. A small dab of diluted white glue will help to prevent fraying on the satin cord ends.

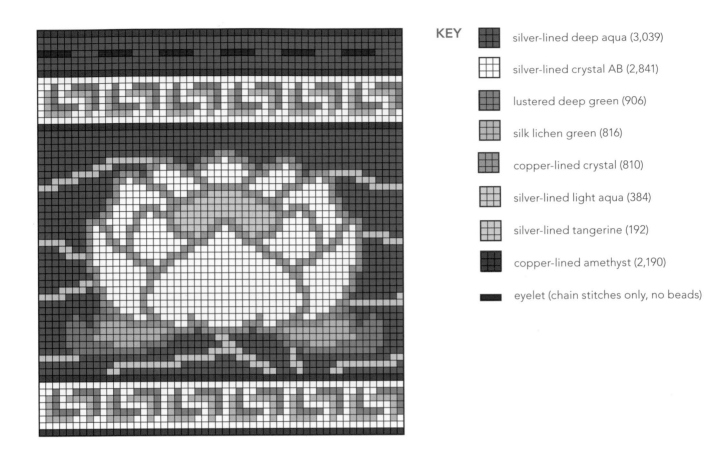

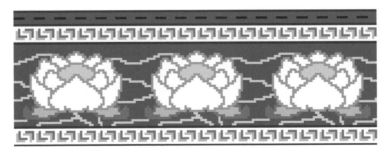

overall pattern of sides

Chapter 6

gusseted patterns

This chapter is filled with projects made using gusseted patterns. They are so simple, yet so elegant.

miss jennie evening bag
golden paisley bag
peacock bag

miss jennie evening bag

Named for my grandmother, a flapper par excellence, this bag brings back the fun and style of a sophisticated era.

before you begin

This piece is crocheted in the round, starting with a rectangular base. The side gussets are only eight stitches wide and are unbeaded; their only function is to support the tubular crochet trim. When you reach the top of the straight side area, you will begin to increase the gusset, which will continue to be unbeaded single crochet. This gusset will disappear into the bag when you finish it. Note that the bead amounts shown below will create the bag itself (no handle or trim) with the paisley pattern on one side and the geometric pattern on the other.

what you need

beads

Total Czech 11° beads for both sides:

 #68106 brass-lined crystal (2,118 beads)

 #57109 silver-lined peridot AB (2,504 beads)

 #57719 silver-lined aqua AB (2,710 beads)

 #39030 amethyst-lined cobalt (1,591 beads)

 #60014 cobalt-lined black (2,027 beads)

Beads for the trim:

 #68106 brass-lined crystal, 30 g

 #57719 silver-lined aqua AB, 10 g

Beads for the handle:

 #68106 brass-lined crystal, 10 g

 #57719 silver-lined aqua AB, 10 g

 #57109 silver-lined peridot AB, 3 g

additional materials and tools

#12 perle cotton, medium dusty blue

30 Czech glass drops, bronze, 4 x 6 mm

60 Japanese magatamas, purple iris, 3 mm

30 Japanese drops, lustered amethyst, 4 mm

Brooch or decorative clasp

Delica 11° #1152, matte rose gold (255 beads)

Nylon beading thread and ordinary sewing thread

Nonwoven stabilizer, 9 x 18 inches (22.9 x 55.9 cm)

Satin or taffeta lining fabric, 9 x 18 inches (22.9 x 55.9 cm)

Polyester quilt batting

Lightweight cardboard (optional)

Crochet hooks, beading needles, and scissors

Sharp hand sewing needles

what you do

1 Create an unbeaded rectangular base, 37 stitches wide by 8 rows deep. (See page 27 for rectangular base instructions.) Cut the thread and secure it within the crochet.

2 Thread on the first section following the charts on pages 102 and 103. Pull up a loop in the fifth single crochet of one of the short sides of the rectangular base. Make four single crochet without beads. Make two single crochet with beads in the next stitch (increase at the corner). Work across the long side of the rectangular base, making one single crochet with a bead in each stitch, except the last, in which you'll make two single crochet with beads (increase at the other corner).

miss jennie evening bag

3 Make eight single crochet without beads along the short side of the rectangular base. Increase in the corner, then work across the long side in single crochet with beads. Increase at the end of that side as well. Make four single crochet without beads in the short side. This will bring you to your starting point. Step up.

4 Work in rounds, continuing as for the first beaded round, increasing at the corners to create the angled edge. Follow the charted design, increasing as indicated, until you reach the straight portion of the design. You'll either be working both the paisley and the geometric sides to make the bag as pictured here or, if you prefer, doing both sides in the same pattern.

tip

If you do decide to make both sides of the bag in the same pattern, you'll need to double the number of beads in each variety given next to the chart for the pattern you've chosen.

threading overview for both sides

5 Work upward in rounds, always making eight unbeaded gusset stitches, until the straight rows are complete.

6 At this point, you'll have 178 stitches in the round; two sections of eight stitches (the gussets) will be unbeaded on opposite sides. Continue with this number of stitches in each round, but start and end your two beaded sections *one stitch inward toward the center* on each successive round. The number of unbeaded stitches will be four more and the number of beaded stitches will be four fewer in each successive round. Gradually, the side gussets will grow and the beaded area will shrink, so a beaded hexagon is formed on both sides along with a wide unbeaded gusset that is wedge-shaped. Continue in this manner until the entire chart is completed. Cut and secure your thread.

7 Use the hexagon as a template to cut two pieces of nonwoven stabilizer. Trim off another ¹/₈ inch (3 mm) all around on both pieces. Baste a layer of polyester batting to each piece of stabilizer; trim the edges. Baste one piece of the stabilizer to each side of the bag, so the batting is between the stabilizer and the back of the crochet.

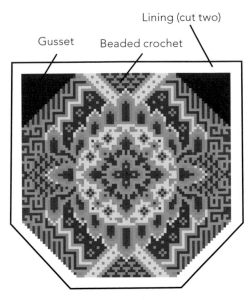

Gusset   Beaded crochet   Lining (cut two)

figure 1

8 Use the hexagon shape as a template to cut two pieces of lining fabric (including the gussets). Allow a ½-inch (1.3 cm) seam margin (see figure 1). Sew a seam along the sides and bottom; press the side seams flat. Fold over the top edge ½ inch (1.3 cm) and press it.

9 Slip the lining inside the bag. Secure it to the top edge of the bag with small invisible stitches, matching the side seams of the lining to the center of the gussets.

make the trim

10 Thread on the brass-lined crystal and silver-lined aqua beads listed for the trim to create the tubular bead crochet trim. The threading pattern is three crystal, one aqua (figure 2). You'll need to create 320 rounds of six stitches to complete each section of trim.

figure 2

11 Follow the instructions on page 24 for tubular bead crochet, working six around to create two tubes that fit neatly around the outside edge of the hexagon. See the pattern in figure 3. When you're satisfied with the fit, join the ends of the tubes invisibly so there are two rings of trim.

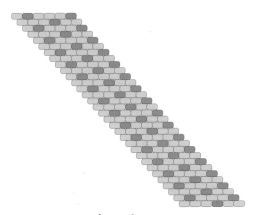

figure 3

tip

The threading required in step 10 adds up to about 20 feet (6.1 m). It's a good idea to make several 5-foot (1.5 m) sections, and join the sections together as you progress. This will be much easier to handle.

miss jennie evening bag

12 Fit the two tubes together around the bottom and sides so they nestle into the un-beaded gusset. Baste the tubes in place with invisible stitches. Now sew the top portion of each ring separately to the top edge of the bag so it lands just at the edge of the lining.

13 Add the decorative trim along the side edges (photo 1). First fit the trim beads into the valley between the two crocheted tubes. Start ½ inch (1.3 cm) down from the top of the straight side. Use ordinary sewing thread or beading nylon of a coordinating color. *Add one magatama, one Japanese drop, one magatama, one Czech drop*. Repeat between *s all around, ending with one magatama, one Japanese drop, one magatama, ½ inch (1.3 cm) from the top of the straight portion on the opposite side.

make the handle

14 The handle is made in tubular bead crochet as well. Use the brass-lined crystal, silver-lined aqua, and silver-lined peridot beads listed for the trim to follow the threading pattern in figure 4. Thread on about 10 feet (3 m) of beads.

figure 4

15 Following the pattern in figure 5, crochet six around until the tube is about 14 inches (35.6 cm) long.

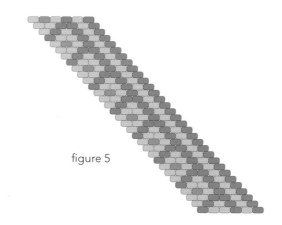
figure 5

1

2

16 Tuck the ends of the tube into the bottom of the gusset, near the top of the straight section (photo 2). Secure the handle in place with several passes of thread.

110

17 Using odd-count peyote stitch, create a strip that is 17 beads wide by 30 rows long (with 15 edge beads). Add silver-lined peridot AB 11° beads to both sides of the strip as shown in figure 6. Add decorations all around in every other row, using light green 11° beads and Japanese drop beads. Wrap the decorated strip around the top center of the handle (see photo 3), and weave the edges of the peyote stitch together to create a tubular decoration. Secure the excess thread within the weave of the peyote and trim.

figure 6

side view

3

miss jennie evening bag

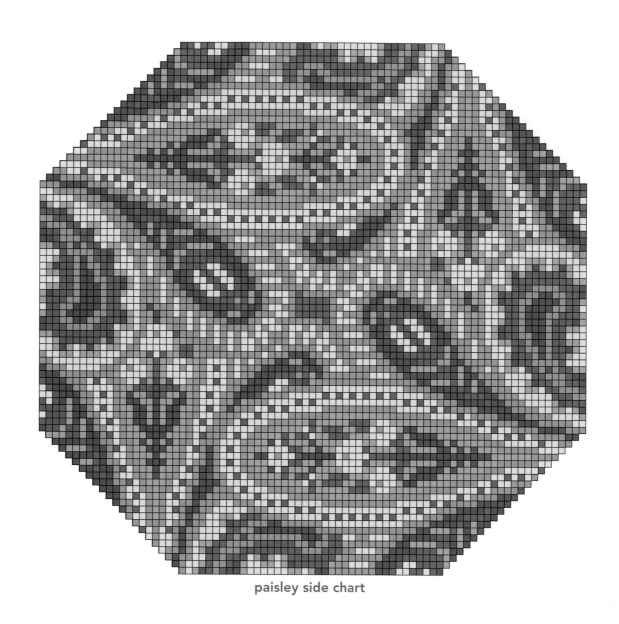

paisley side chart

KEY

#68106 brass-lined crystal (1,318)

#57109 silver-lined peridot AB (828)

#57719 silver-lined aqua AB (1,612)

#39030 amethyst-lined cobalt (819)

#60014 cobalt-lined black (898)

geometric side chart

KEY  #68106 brass-lined crystal (800)

#57109 silver-lined peridot AB (1676)

#57719 silver-lined aqua AB (1,098)

#39030 amethyst-lined cobalt (772)

#60014 cobalt-lined black (1,129)

The colors of this paisley design work together brilliantly—in every sense. The gold of the bag's top and clasp is reflected in a number of the beads, especially those 15° beads outlining the edge. All the bag's colors come together in its rainbow of a rope handle.

golden paisley bag

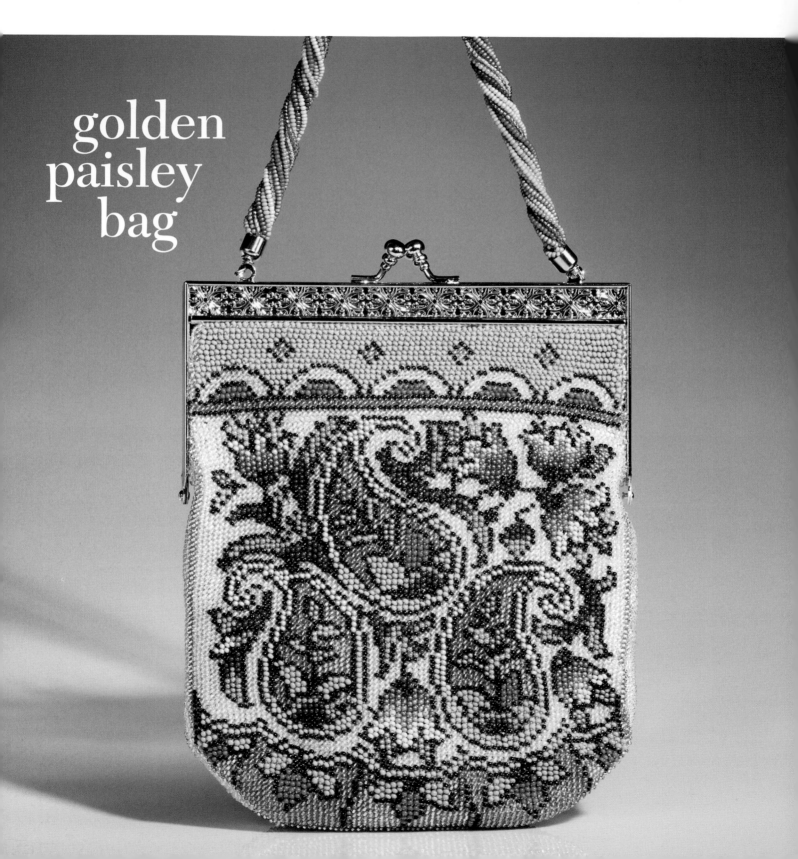

golden paisley bag

before you begin

In this project you'll use a panoply of techniques. You start with a rectangular base, then build the bag off the base with side increases for the first 15 rounds. Near the top, you switch to back-and-forth stitching so you can attach the bag to a metal-hinged clasp. Finally, you make a twisted bead rope handle with all the bead colors. One special threading note: For each fuchsia square in the stitch chart, you'll be threading on three 15° beads. When stitching, bring all three down the thread and catch them in one stitch. This will create a sharper corner than if only one bead was used in that place.

what you need

beads (for two sides)

Bead count is for the two sides, rectangular base, and gusset. For the handle, add 160 beads of each color.

All Czech 11° seed beads:

 #17020 silver-lined light gold
(712 beads)

 #89010 silver-lined topaz
(914 beads)

 #23580 silk light olive
(456 beads)

 #54430 opaque olive
(2,102 beads)

 #63020 opaque light blue
(424 beads)

 #33210 opaque marine blue
(370 beads)

 #23720 silk pale pink
(310 beads)

 #23940 silk medium pink
(294 beads)

 #BL568 silk rose
(302 beads)

 #28020 lustered light amethyst
(406 beads)

 #23040 opaque amethyst
(460 beads)

 #58200 lustered bright green
(184 beads)

 #25511 silk dark sage
(244 beads)

 #48102 lustered transparent crystal
(4,674 beads)

 #23980 opaque black
(4,910 beads)

additional materials and tools

 Matsuno #32 15°, silver-lined gold
(832 beads)

#12 perle cotton, bisque color, 20 g

Metal-hinged clasp with sew holes, 5½ to 6 inches (14 to 15.2 cm) long

Strong nylon thread for sewing bag to handle

22-gauge brass wire, two 4-inch (10.2 cm) pieces

2 bead caps, ³⁄8 inch (9.5 mm) diameter

Crochet hooks, beading needles, and scissors

White glue

Wire cutters

Pliers

what you do

1 Following the directions on page 27, create a rectangular base. The initial chain for the base is 52 stitches. Work until the base is 10 rows deep and 53 beads wide. Break your thread; pull it through the last loop and secure it in the crochet.

2 Following the stitch chart on page 119, thread on beads in sections of six or seven rows. You should thread straight across in horizontal rows and also connect straight across chart gaps. Thread each diagram row twice to make a two-sided bag. (See the overview on page 116). For each fuchsia square, thread on three 15° silver-lined gold beads.

golden paisley bag

3 The rectangular base forms the bottom of the bag. The short sides of the rectangular base, when continued upward as you crochet the pattern, will form the side gussets. The gussets will then have beads on each side. To begin creating the sides, attach your thread in the center of one of the sides of the rectangular base, so there are five stitches to the corner in that side. Crochet the five gusset beads to the corner. In the corner stitch, make two stitches, one that has three 15° beads, and one that has the first bead of the pattern (see photo 1). Crochet with beads across the row. After the last pattern bead, crochet three 15° beads in the same space to make the increase. Crochet the gusset beads until you reach the corner again, then repeat as for the other side of the bag.

4 Continue working in rounds, stepping up at the center of one gusset (see photo 1 again), until you reach the back-and-forth section. Following the top of the chart, thread the rows back and forth. Crochet using the back-and-forth technique, decreasing as needed. Crochet both sides of the bag the same.

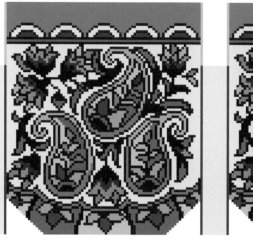

threading overview

finish the bag

5 Secure all tail threads within the crochet and trim them. Attach the metal clasp to the bag by sewing with the nylon thread. Secure the threads inside with one bead; make two passes of thread through each bead if possible (see photo 2).

Anchoring beads

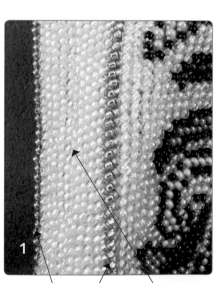

Step-up in center of gusset

Three-bead corner

6 Make one 14-inch (35.6 cm) strand of each color of 11° bead; leave thread ends of 4 inches (10.2 cm) on both ends of each strand. Gather one end of all the strands together and tie a tight knot. Compress all the beads together so there is no slack on the threads; remove or add beads as necessary to create even strands. Tie a knot in the other side, making sure there are no visible threads. Trim both ends to 1 inch (2.5 cm) long (photo 3).

7 Glue the knots at the ends of the strap (photo 4). Bend each section of the brass wire in half. At each end, loop a wire section through the bead strands inside the knot (photo 5).

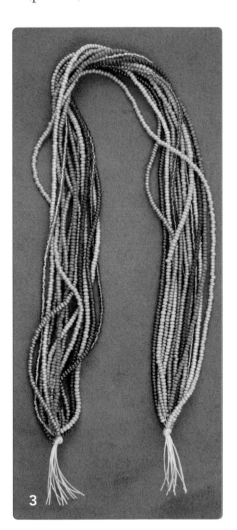

8 Slip one of the bead caps in place over the two wires at each end (photo 6). Make a bend and slip the doubled wire through the handle hole (photo 7).

9 Twist the wire around itself on one side until secure; trim with wire cutters. Twist the rope tightly, and hold the position so the twist remains as you attach the other end of the handle to the hole (photo 8).

Thread straight
across in
horizontal rows

Connect straight
across chart gaps

Add three 15°s in the fuchsia spaces along the edges of the main
design area—the sixth row in from both left and right.

KEY

silver-lined light gold (712)	opaque marine blue (370)	opaque amethyst (460)
silver-lined topaz (914)	silk pale pink (310)	lustered bright green (184)
silk light olive (456)	silk medium pink (294)	silk dark sage (244)
opaque olive (2,102)	silk rose (302)	lustered transparent crystal (4,674)
opaque light blue (424)	lustered light amethyst (406)	opaque black (4,910)

peacock bag

Pretty as a peacock?
That's this elegant bag.
Proud as a peacock? That's
you after you've made it.

peacock bag

before you begin

The lower portion of this over-the-wrist bag is worked in the round, building on a rectangular base. This section has a 20-stitch gusset on both sides. The upper portion is worked back and forth in two separate sections, which are joined at the top to form a self-handle. You create the raised line of metallic bronze that defines its edges by stitching three 15° beads in place of one 11° bead. No lining is required.

what you need

beads

Czech 11° beads (unless otherwise noted):

 #10024 black-lined topaz (12,780 beads)

 Toho #223 15°, metallic bronze (2,436 beads)

Thread three for each square.

 #23980 opaque black (552 beads)

 #37100 silver-lined dark cobalt (1,344 beads)

 #57719 silver-lined aqua AB (1,170 beads)

 #68130 lustered opaque green-aqua (1,094 beads)

 #57229 brass-lined lime AB (3,804 beads)

 #57109 silver-lined peridot AB (2,164 beads)

Note: Each square in the stitch chart for Toho #223 metallic bronze represents three beads threaded on, and red squares in the chart are threaded with #10024 black-lined topaz.

additional materials and tools

#12 perle cotton, mustard color

2 matching wooden handles, painted gold

Crochet hooks, beading needles, and scissors

what you do

1 Following the general directions for rectangular bases on page 27, create a rectangular base of 11° black-lined topaz beads, 35 stitches wide and 20 rows deep.

make the lower portion

2 Following the Lower Portion chart on page 124, thread on the first section. (See the Threading Overview illustration on page 123 to see how the parts of the bag fit together.) Start with 10 black-lined topaz beads; this represents half the gusset on one side. When threading on the Toho 15° beads, each square on the chart represents three beads. Each threaded section will start and end with 10 black-lined topaz beads, so the step-up will land in the center of one of the gussets.

3 Hold the rectangular base with the beads facing away from you. Count 11 stitches up from the lower right corner. (Left-handed stitchers should count up from the lower left corner.) Pull up your loop in this stitch. Chain one, then single crochet with a bead in the same stitch. Make nine more single crochet with beads. In the next stitch, work two stitches, each one having three Toho 15° metallic bronze beads (corner increase). Work across the top of the rectangular base, working three 15° beads into each stitch. In the corner stitch, work two three-bead stitches (corner increase).

peacock bag

4 Work down the side of the gusset with 20 single crochet with bead. In the corner stitch, work two three-bead stitches, then work across the other side of the rectangular base with single crochet, again with each stitch having three 15° beads. Increase at the corner again, then work up the side with single crochet with one bead each. Step up at the center of the gusset.

5 Following the chart, work upward in rounds, increasing at the sides of the front and back as indicated by making two stitches in each of the three-bead corner stitches. On the right side of the both front and back, you'll make the stitch with three 15° beads first, followed by the stitch with one 11° bead. On the left side, you'll make the stitch with one 11° bead first, then the stitch with three 15° beads. (Left-handed stitchers should reverse this.)

6 In the straight sections of the lower portion of the bag, don't make increases; simply stitch each stitch with three 15° beads into the stitch with three 15° beads of the previous round. A nice corner will develop.

7 When the pattern calls for decreases, pull up three loops (as shown in the general directions on page 18) and make one stitch with three 15° beads. Continue stitching until the lower portion is complete. Cut and secure your thread.

8 Make four-row unbeaded hems in the gusset section of both sides of the lower portion by working back and forth in the 20 stitches of 11° beads. Don't make a hem within the front and back sections.

make the upper portion

9 Thread on the lowest section of the upper portion of the bag. Remember that you're threading on only one side at a time, as shown in the threading overview.

10 Join one side of the upper portion to the lower portion at the red squares in the chart. Work back and forth until the entire section is complete. Leave a long thread tail to use later.

11 Work the other side of the upper portion in the same manner.

finish

12 Wrap each top edge of the upper portion around one of the wooden handles and make seams to enclose the handles.

13 Stitch the hems in place within the gussets.

14 Pinch the corner together in the place where the upper section meets the lower section; using invisible stitches, make a small tuck to better define the gusset at the meeting point of the two portions.

When the back and forth section is complete, secure the thread within the crochet and trim it. On a new thread, load fifty-one 15°s, and crochet one three-bead stitch into the end of each horizontal row. Do this on all four side edges of the upper portions.

Wrap the upper portion around the shaft of your handle and secure the last row to the crochet stitches on the inside of the bag, in a straight line. When the handle is attached, secure the thread and trim it.

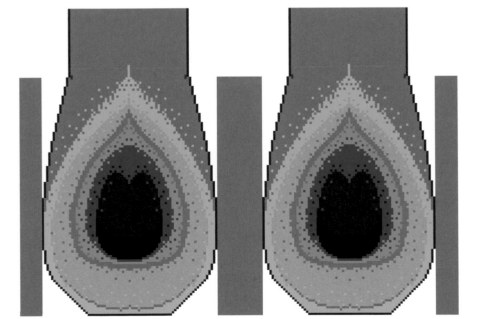

lower portion chart

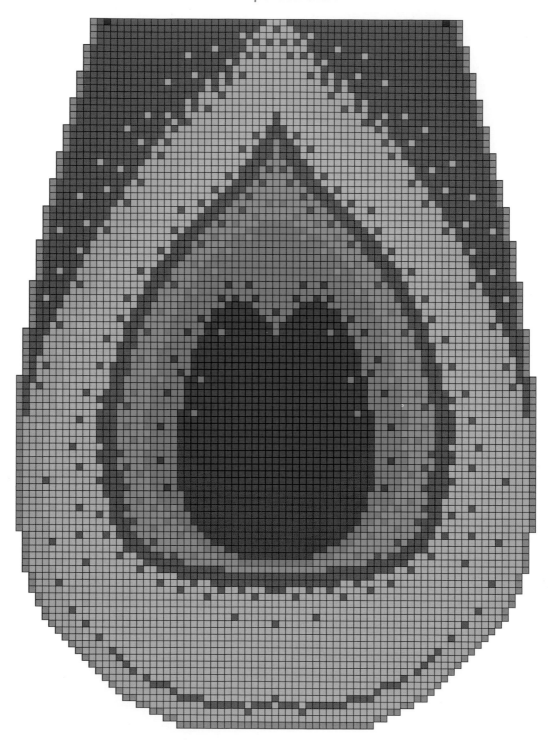

KEY for lower portion chart (bead counts are for entire bag)

black-lined topaz (12,780)

15° metallic bronze (2,436)

Note: Each square in the chart for 15° metallic bronze represents three beads threaded on.

opaque black (552)

silver-lined dark cobalt (1,344)

silver-lined aqua AB (1,170)

lustered opaque green-aqua (1,094)

brass-lined lime AB (3,804)

silver-lined peridot AB (2,164)

black-lined topaz

upper portion chart

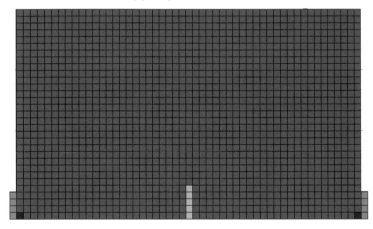

KEY

black-lined topaz (12,780)

15° metallic bronze (2,436)

silver-lined peridot AB

design charts

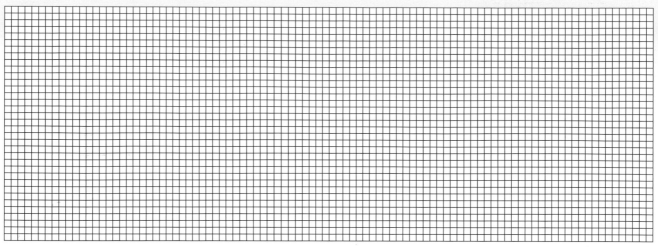

TREASURE BOX

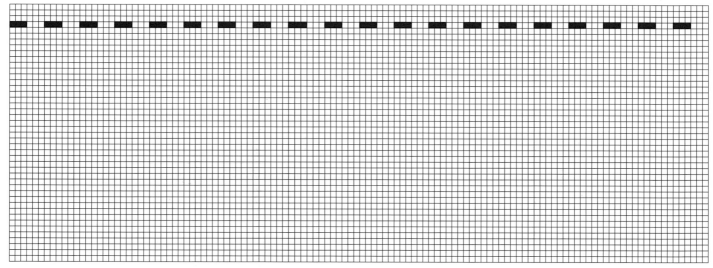

PINEAPPLE DRAWSTRING BAG

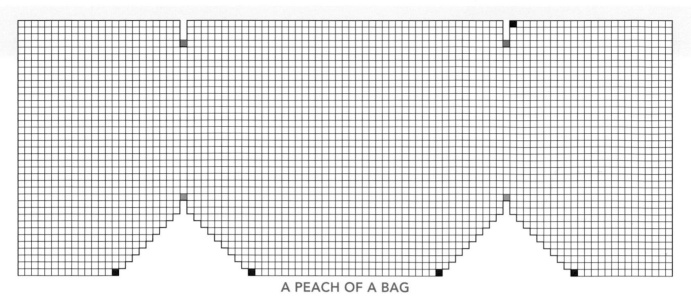

A PEACH OF A BAG

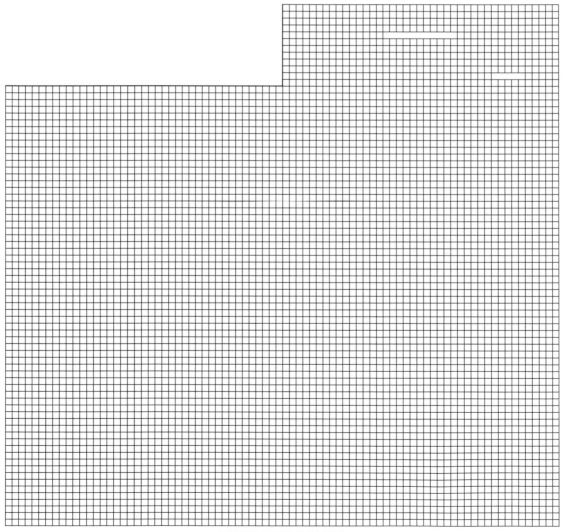

LISTEN UP! POUCH

index

about the author

Ann Benson is the author of eight books on beadwork; she specializes in bead crochet. She is the owner of Beads East store in Connecticut and www.beadseast.com online. She has taught beading and lectured widely on graphics applications used in writing beadwork directions. She is also the author of four novels, *The Plague Tales*, *The Burning Road*, *The Physician's Tale*, and *Thief of Souls*.

She is married to Gary Frost, with whom she shares homes in Connecticut and Florida. Ann is the mother of two grown daughters, who are her best work ever.

acknowledgments

Thanks to Renee Frost, Carolyn Reese, and Sharol Ellis for their wonderful assistance in stringing and stitching. Thanks especially to Lauren Miller, who contributed two exquisite designs to this collection, which was much improved by their inclusion. Special loving thanks to Gary Frost for vacuuming up all those discarded paper markers. Thanks to Mom for teaching me how to crochet when I was eight years old.

abbreviations and equivalents

ch = chain stitch

chb = chain stitch with a bead

sl st = slip stitch

sc = single crochet

scb = single crochet with a bead

1 gram of Czech 11° beads = about 100 beads

1 gram of Japanese 11° beads = about 90 beads

1 gram of Japanese 15° beads = about 275 beads

1 hank of Czech beads = about 34 grams

1 inch = about 2.5 cm

1 meter = about 39 inches